Lending

TRACING YOUR

County Council

Libraries, books and more . . .

Please return/renew this item by the last due date.
Library items may also be renewed by phone or
via our website.
www.cumbria.gov.uk/libra~

Cumbria Libraries

CLIC

Interactive Catalogue

Ask for a CLIC passwor

D1514328

TRACING YOUR NORTHERN ANCESTORS

A Guide to the North-East and Cumbria for the Family Historian

KEITH GREGSON

Pen & Sword
FAMILY HISTORY

First published in Great Britain in 2007 by
PEN & SWORD FAMILY HISTORY
an imprint of
Pen & Sword Books Ltd
47 Church Street
Barnsley
South Yorkshire
S70 2AS

Unless otherwise stated, photographs are from the Author's collection.

ISBN 978 1 84415 597 2

A CIP catalogue record for this book is
available from the British Library.

Typeset in Palatino and Optima by
Phoenix Typesetting, Auldgirth, Dumfriesshire

Printed and bound in England by
CPI UK

Pen & Sword Books Ltd incorporates the Imprints of
Pen & Sword Aviation, Pen & Sword Maritime, Pen & Sword Military,
Wharncliffe Local History, Pen & Sword Select, Pen & Sword Military
Classics and Leo Cooper.

For a complete list of Pen & Sword titles please contact
PEN & SWORD BOOKS LIMITED
47 Church Street, Barnsley, South Yorkshire, S70 2AS, England
E-mail: enquiries@pen-and-sword.co.uk
Website: www.pen-and-sword.co.uk

CONTENTS

Preface   vii

Introduction to the Region   1

Section One: Work in the North Country   **15**

Chapter One   Mining   17
Chapter Two   Shipbuilding   31
Chapter Three   Agriculture   43
Chapter Four   Iron and Steel Manufacture and Engineering   51
Chapter Five   Transport   59
Chapter Six   Other Industries   73

Section Two: North Country Life   **81**

Chapter Seven   Religion   83
Chapter Eight   National Government   94
Chapter Nine   Local Government   98
Chapter Ten   Military and Warfare   105
Chapter Eleven   Education   117
Chapter Twelve   Dialect and Diet   124
Chapter Thirteen   Leisure   129

Section Three: Movement   **139**

Chapter Fourteen   Movement   141

Appendixes: Research Guide   **151**

Appendix One   Archives, Libraries and Local Studies Centres   153
Appendix Two   Web Resources   169
Appendix Three   Other Useful Organisations and Resources   172
Appendix Four   Museums and Heritage Centres   174

Select Bibliography   192

Index   195

This book is dedicated to the memory of Gill Shirvinton (1954–2006)
– a real North Country Lass in every respect.

A North Country maid
Up To London had strayed
Although with her nature, it did not agree
She wept and she cried
Then she rang her hands and sighed
How I wish once again in the north I could be

Where the oak and the ash
And the bonny ivy tree
They are all growing greener
In my North Country

(As taught at St George's Primary School, Kendal *c*.1955)

PREFACE

Writing about ancestry in a region as widespread as the far north of England is not an easy task; even definition of its geographical boundaries can cause a headache.

The region, as presented here, stretches from the Anglo-Scottish border in the north to areas round the northern borders of the ancient counties of Lancashire and Yorkshire in the south. Its western flank runs from the Morecambe Bay estuary up the western coast along the southern coastline of the Solway Firth to the western end of the Scottish border. The eastern boundary runs from the eastern end of the Scottish border to an area just south of the River Tees.

Using the current political arrangements, this includes Cumbria in the North-West, Modern County Durham and Northumberland, Tyneside, Wearside and the Tees Valley in the North-East.

This is a region with which I am very familiar despite a birth registered in London (where I subsequently lived for a few months). Otherwise I am in every sense a North Country man, driven perhaps by the accident of my birth into a search for my northern roots.

Both my mother and my father's father started life in Barrow-in-Furness (Cumbria), where my father was also brought up. My mother's father was born in Millom (Cumbria) and his wife in South Shields (Tyneside). My own early years were spent in Kendal and my teenage years in Carlisle (both Cumbria). I then crossed the Pennines to go to university in Newcastle (Tyneside), taught history in Hartlepool (Tees Valley) and have lived in Sunderland (Wearside) for over thirty years. My oldest son is now settled in Alnwick (Northumberland), while my mother and other close relatives are on the south Solway coast (still Cumbria).

Although I reckon this is a good pedigree for someone writing about the North Country and ancestry, I am aware of a tendency to draw on evidence and examples connected to those places with which I am most familiar. I hope that this doesn't blur the broader picture and that fellow family historians can draw on the examples I use to achieve success where their own geographical areas of interest differ slightly from mine.

As a songwriter, I was tempted, some years ago, to put my love of my 'almost native' land into verse. The chorus ended:

> *Of Kendal and Carlisle, Tweed, Tees, Wear and Tyne*
> *Of the mountains, the lakes and the moorlands so fine*
> *From the backbone of England see a country of mine*
> *Which I wouldn't exchange for another*

This may be slightly treacherous coming from one with Wembley written in large letters on his birth certificate but it is true nevertheless.

With any luck, what follows may assist 'fellow northerners', firmly rooted or not, to discover their ancestors and, equally importantly, in my estimation, to build up a picture of how they may have lived, worked and played.

Keith Gregson
Sunderland
2007

INTRODUCTION TO THE REGION

If you are not familiar with the north of England, you will probably be unaware of the controversial nature of the title of this book – and there are a number of issues here. First, some will want to know how there can be a book with 'Northern' in the title that does not deal with modern Lancashire or Yorkshire? The answer is simple. This book is one in a series of guides where these two counties will stand on their own. As they are geographically 'south' of the region which includes both the North-East and Cumbria then there is no harm in that region becoming exclusively 'Northern'. Second, the placing of the North-East and Cumbria under one umbrella may raise a few eyebrows. This is not necessary. The media recognises this region, both in television and newspaper coverage. There is also a natural unity across the region, which should become more evident later in the book.

Take the 'Roman Wall' or Hadrian's Wall, for example, constructed almost two thousand years ago. Commonly regarded as marking the fixed northern limit of the Roman Empire, it stretched from the Solway in the west almost to the mouth of the Tyne in the east. Although it was a frontier rather than an effective fortified barrier, its influence and area of protection stretched southwards for a considerable distance.

Later, as the medieval period came to a close, the Scottish border as we now know it began to be fixed in place. Prior to this, the whole area had been wild, and a common fear of attack from north of the border gave it a form of unity. Hartlepool, on the south-eastern fringe of the region, was frequently raided by Scots, and at least one Westmorland market-town in the far south-west (Kirkby Stephen) had its streets developed specifically in a pattern to keep out such invaders.

Even as the border fell into place in the sixteenth century, this remained a difficult region to govern, as families and their feuds reigned supreme. The official law was overseen in three marches: the Western Marches, based on Carlisle, the Middle, based on Hexham, and the Eastern, based on Newcastle. Although officials here frequently failed to see eye to eye, the enemy was often a common one throughout the great days of the border reivers, or rustlers.

So this is 'The North', signposted all the way up the A1 and M6 until it disappears into Scotland, also described as 'the Far North' or even, for simplicity, the North Country. 'North Country' is certainly a phrase used of the region, or parts of it, in times past. It appears in songs such as 'The North Country Maid', one of the most common versions of which is tied directly to the southern part of modern Cumbria.

It was also in common use among sailors in the nineteenth century when they talked of gatherings of 'North Country vessels' in foreign ports.

Be this as it may, the most likely starting point for the modern family historian is at an archive somewhere in a specific part of the region as it is organised in the twenty-first century. Through this structure (which encompasses the record offices, museums, libraries and heritage centres), the region's often complex past history and organisation can best be understood.

Where geographical structure is required in this book, it will start in the west with Cumbria and follow round in a clockwise direction until the Tees Valley is reached in the south-east of the region.

Cumbria

The ancient roots of the modern county of Cumbria are spread far and wide. The county itself was actually set up in 1974, formed from the former counties of Cumberland and Westmorland plus the Furness district of Lancashire and the Sedbergh district of Yorkshire. Today it might be conveniently divided into five areas of influence although boundaries are, in some cases, indistinct. These areas are North Cumbria, West Cumbria, the Lake District, the Furness area and Rough Fell Country.

North Cumbria is centred on Carlisle – an historic city if ever there was one. Once a significant Roman town, it has a castle and a cathedral that have seen it all. National parliaments were held here, and Oliver Cromwell, Mary Queen of Scots and Bonnie Prince Charlie all feature in its history. It was also an industrial city, once home to the production of metal boxes and fabrics, and still remains one of the United Kingdom's most significant railway centres. It is also, in a sense, a large market-town, drawing people in from north of the border, the Solway coast and the old John Peel hunting country, which stretches towards the Lake District. Brampton, situated towards the east and the Northumbrian border, is also an influential North Cumbrian market-town.

West Cumbria revolves around the major towns of Workington and Whitehaven and stretches north to the Solway estuary and south to Millom. This is another area of considerable historical interest. In the eighteenth century, Whitehaven, in particular, prospered due to its west coast links to Ireland and the American colonies, and its success was, at one time, a very real threat to the merchants of Liverpool. Millom, Workington and Whitehaven all benefited from the developments in iron- and coal-mining and iron and steel manufacture in the nineteenth century. In the twentieth century it was the turn of chemicals and, more controversially, nuclear energy, with the names of Calder Hall and Windscale (now known as Sellafield) nationally known.

The Lake District is generally considered to stretch from the southern tip of Windermere to the northern tip of Bassenthwaite; from Ennerdale in the west to the eastern tip of Ullswater. Often seen as a 'more manageable' Switzerland in terms of size, its tentacles also snake across the fells towards Kendal and south through Cartmel to Grange-over-Sands. Cartmel once had an influential little priory; today it is known for its tourism and popular race meetings. Grange-over-Sands looks over towards the more popular resorts of Blackpool, Morecambe and Heysham, and long possessed the reputation of a rather genteel watering-hole.

Although generally manageable in size, the Lake District is made up of parts of the former counties of Cumberland and Westmorland, and Lancashire, and has centres of population at Cockermouth and Keswick in the north and Windermere, Ambleside and Coniston to the south. Cockermouth guards the far northern exit from Lakeland and is a bustling market-town with historic links to the Wordsworth family. Keswick, Windermere and Ambleside (and, to some extent, Grasmere) form the spine of the tourist's Lake District, often disguising a long and interesting industrial heritage. Noted for its agriculture as well as its tourism, 'The Lakes' has been home to significant industries over the years, including mining for slate, graphite and copper.

The Furness area radiates out from Barrow-in-Furness as far as the southern Lakes, even extending to the M6 motorway. The railway was introduced into the town to carry iron ore, slate and limestone to its new deep-water port. Barrow itself was once a large industrial town, growing from a tiny nineteenth-century hamlet to a very big iron and steel centre and a major shipbuilding force. The population grew from 300 inhabitants to over 8,000 in 1864 with both the Ramsden and Cavendish families making significant contributions to building up the heavy industries.

Ulverston and Dalton are also sizeable centres of population in the Furness area. The remainder of the county, including some central areas but mainly eastern and south-eastern areas, is now happy to recognise its historical links with sheep and the wool trade and markets itself under the banner of 'Rough Fell Country'. This incorporates centres of population such as Sedbergh, Kirkby Stephen, Kirkby Lonsdale and Appleby. Sedbergh is home to a public school famed for prowess at sport; the others are market-towns of considerable character.

Rough Fell Country stretches as far as the former metal mining town of Alston in the east and, in particular, into Penrith and Kendal. Penrith was the marketing centre for the southern part of the former county of Cumberland and an important crossroads between east and west. It marks the main entrance to the northern Lakes from the east. Kendal was the industrial centre of the former county of Westmorland with a reputation for its shoes, woollen products and mint cake.

Although it is difficult to encapsulate this essentially rural county by reference to a single place, the North Cumbrian village of Burgh-by-Sands on the

Solway may serve the purpose. In the 1820s, villagers made candlewick and linen cloth, and many women quilted. There were tobacco producers and maltsters, weavers, shoemakers, smiths, carpenters and of course farmers and agricultural workers (even today there are working farms at the very heart of the village).

As there are today, there were Hodgsons galore, then distinguished by place of residence such as 'Buckbottom', 'Cross' and 'Paddock Hole' or, in other cases, by more intimate and less flattering nicknames such as 'blue-nebbed Watt' and 'ewe-chinned Dick'!

Northumberland

Modern Northumberland thrives on tourism and heritage and is a county difficult to describe without using the language of the tourist guide. This basically rural county occupies the former Middle and Eastern Marches of the English border; in consequence the population lies clustered around centres initially developed for either defence or marketing agricultural produce.

In the county's deep south-west, Allendale and Allenhead (possibly exceptions to the cluster rule) overlook moors once teeming with metal mines. From the Cumbrian border, Tynedale (or the Tynedales, as the North Tyne, South Tyne and Tyne rivers exist separately) sweep the visitor on towards Newcastle in the south and Berwick to the north. Key communities here are Haltwhistle, Haydon Bridge and Hexham, which was the Saxon capital of Hexhamshire, home to some of the first monastic lands in England. The town proves a central draw with its ancient abbey and functional market place. It was also the administrative centre of the English Middle March and has a long and often bloody history. Nearby Ovingham boasts an ancient goose fair and Cherryburn was home to the great engraver Thomas Bewick. Corbridge, the Roman Corstopitum, was built at a major crossroads and remains well known to modern travellers.

Northwards lies Otterburn, site of a famous battle in medieval times while Bellingham was at the heart of reiver country. Running across the area is the great Kielder Forest and its twentieth-century reservoir. The area of Northumberland just north of Newcastle and stretching inland from the coast shows greater signs of industrialisation and urbanisation. Blyth was a port of some significance in the nineteenth century, and Ashington the centre of a coal-mining district. Just north of Newcastle itself new towns and industries were established at Cramlington and Bedlington.

Moving northwards from Newcastle up the 'Great North Road' there are three areas of influence – Morpeth, Alnwick and Berwick. Morpeth, home to Collingwood, hero of Trafalgar, remains a busy market-town and dormitory for Newcastle. Its folk retain a great sense of heritage and there is an annual gathering to celebrate this. Alnwick lies slightly further north and is home to the Dukes of Northumberland, the Percy family of 'Hotspur' fame. The town's fine castle is much used in feature films and overlooks fields where an annual Shrovetide football match is still played. A twenty-first century poll recently declared Alnwick to be the most desirable place in England to live!

Within easy reach of Alnwick are the fishing villages of Craster, Seahouses and Alnmouth. Close by, too, reminding us of the age of warfare, lie the abandoned castles at Dunstanburgh and Warkworth. Just to the north are Bamburgh and Holy Island (Lindisfarne), places of considerable history.

Towards the border there are further fortified settlements, notably Ford and Etal, and Berwick-upon-Tweed's significance is such that it is considered the eastern equivalent of the Border City of Carlisle. Berwick has a famously chequered history – its football team actually plays in the Scottish League – and the town has seen such turmoil that, according to local legend, it remained for a long time officially at war with Russia after a legal oversight left it out of a peace treaty.

Northumberland is an appropriate place for the pursuit of family history: it was one of the major areas where family often took precedence over all other social groupings. As in the clan system north of the border, there was family unity in Northumberland, and maps are now available which show the exact areas in which those with famous border names such as Forster, Charlton and Ridley lived. Close to Berwick were the haunts of the Selbys, Herons, Grays and Chamberlains. The Ridleys could be found around the South Tyne, the Fenwicks north of Newcastle and Hexham.

The three great football names of Charlton, Robson and Milburn have their roots in the wilds of the North Tyne Valley. For many of these families, protection and defence were crucial, and these created unique bonds. As in areas of Cumbria and southern Scotland, ruined pele towers and fortified farmhouses are common features of the landscape. As peace came to the area, agriculture, coal production and sea-related work became the order of the day.

Tyneside

The term 'Tyneside' is as difficult to define as the much-used yet equally controversial term 'Geordie'. One easy escape might be to simply describe a 'Geordie' as a 'Tynesider' or vice versa and hope to get away with it. Thankfully the changes in local government have helped slightly in providing a solution to the problem.

The former Tyne and Wear is now a rump organisation servicing museums, the fire brigade and the postal organisation; the strictly Tyne or Tyneside elements within its boundaries consist of Newcastle upon Tyne, North Tyneside, South Tyneside and Gateshead. The boundaries of these four elements can thus be taken as marking the limits of modern Tyneside.

The City Walls - a reminder of Newcastle's turbulent past.

At the heart of Tyneside lies the City of Newcastle upon Tyne. Its origins are to be found around the original Roman bridge which lay close to the site of modern Tyne Bridge; the early settlement grew around this bridge, the river, castle and cathedral. By the eighteenth century, Newcastle was firmly established as a regional capital; the Georgian period carried the city further up the bank and nineteenth-century legislation widened its bounds even further. Byker, Walker, Kenton, Denton, Elswick, Jesmond and Gosforth are among its better-known suburbs today.

Within these confines were to be found all the industries associated with Tyneside – shipbuilding (both naval and merchant), coal production, pottery, glass and armaments.

Gateshead lies immediately across the river from Newcastle and has, in years past, suffered from its proximity to its better-known neighbour. At a meeting of the local poor-law guardians of Gateshead in the nineteenth century, one speaker complained that they had no 'villa-rich' ratepayers to pay for the problems of the poor although parts of Gateshead's Victorian suburb of Low Fell were quite prosperous. Gateshead also had all the trappings of a successful Victorian town in its art gallery, its municipal buildings and Saltwell Park. Gateshead folk, like those across the water, worked the river and produced coal and were involved in most of the heavy industries associated with the region.

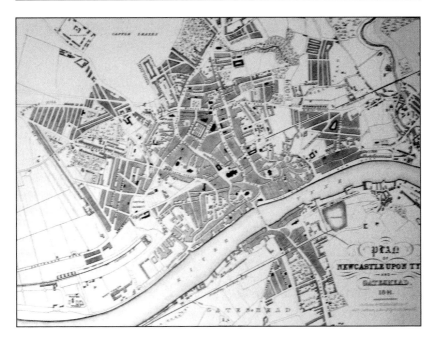

Ancient map of Newcastle.

North Tyneside has the coast and the river as two of its boundaries, and includes the former fishing port of North Shields and Tynemouth with its ancient castle and abbey. To the west is Wallsend, once famed for coal and shipbuilding and, as its very name suggests, constituting the eastern end of Hadrian's Wall. Cullercoats, on the coast, has links with fishing and holiday-making, and Whitley Bay has long been a mecca for tourists.

Across the river lies South Tyneside, centred on the borough of South Shields. Like its northern neighbour, sea and river bound it on two sides. Despite being separated by the Tyne, there is togetherness about 'the folks of Shields', North and South, which has led to local tales and anecdotes passed down from generation to generation. South Shields was an important port and early shipbuilding town with links back to Roman times when, as Arbeia, it was a provisioning centre for troops on Hadrian's Wall. Also in South Tyneside are the towns of Hebburn and Jarrow. Jarrow is well known for its march of the unemployed to London in the 1930s and also for Palmer's shipyard.

South of South Shields and dovetailing into Wearside are the Boldons (East Boldon, West Boldon and the former Boldon Colliery). Although the North Country failed to feature in the Domesday Book, the local Boldon Book has

Wallsend looks to its Roman past.

made up for this in a small way. This was completed in the twelfth century and was basically a survey of all the estates then belonging to the bishopric of Durham.

Towards the coast lies Whitburn, its immediate area linked historically to fishing and coal production.

Although there can be no such thing as a 'typical' Victorian Tyneside family, the Ridleys who produced the songwriter Geordie, writer of 'The Blaydon Races', provide an interesting case. In the 1851 census, Geordie, living in Gateshead, was described as a miner; ten years later as a vocalist. In the same two census returns, members of the family were recorded as rope-maker, blacksmith, ostler, apprentice to bread-baker, cartman, iron moulder, wire rope-maker and plain labourer.

An interesting sideline for the family historian here is that Geordie's brother Stephen Ridley (christened Stephenson Ridley, after his mother's family) later gained local and national fame as the one-mile athletic running champion of England.

Tyneside ancestors may also have been involved in other key industries involving the production of glass and iron and the collection of salt (see section 1, Work in the North Country).

Wearside

The terms 'Wearside' and 'Wearsiders' are ones frequently used and fairly well understood in North-East England. They refer almost exclusively to the territory and people of the lower reaches of the River Wear close to the North Sea. Today Wearside effectively consists of the City of Sunderland. It remains in the larger county of Durham for sporting purposes only and retains a Tyne and Wear postcode as a reminder of its past links with the largely defunct 'twentieth-century county'.

Thirty years ago Sunderland was a town with a polytechnic; now it is a city with a university and fast metro links to the heart of neighbouring Tyneside. The city surrounds the mouth and last stages of the River Wear with its main Wearmouth Bridge linking the key ancient parish of Monkwearmouth in the north to Bishopwearmouth in the south.

The current city centre lies in Bishopwearmouth parish, which traditionally extended southwards and contained the townships of Bishopwearmouth, Bishopwearmouth Panns, Burdon, Ford, Silksworth, Tunstall and Ryhope. Monkwearmouth was made up of Monkwearmouth, Monkwearmouth shore, Fulwell, Southwick and Hylton townships to the north.

The original parish of Sunderland is to the east and lies slightly south of the river-mouth. It was once heaving with homes and places of work, but is now somewhat abandoned. Nevertheless it is here, close to work, the river and the sea, that the story of many Sunderland ancestors is to be found.

The small, yet far from insignificant, former mining communities of Houghton-le-Spring and Hetton-le-Hole dominate the western fringes of the borough. These in turn attract inhabitants of other, smaller, former mining communities such as Eppleton and Penshaw.

Last, but far from least in terms of importance, is the twentieth-century 'new town' of Washington; based on an ancient settlement with close links to the USA, for centuries it was home for the Wessington ancestors of the first president of the United States. Although noted for its new buildings, shops, homes and businesses, Washington still has within its boundaries the remnants of declined mining communities such as Concorde and Usworth.

In the twenty-first century, Wearside is almost exclusively urban, containing one or two scattered farms and some areas of recovered mining land. As in many modern conurbations, it is becoming increasingly difficult to judge where one community now ends and another begins. The story of Wearside is one of shipbuilding, shipping and coal along with a few other trades and industries.

Historians earmark the seventeenth century as a key one in the development of the then town and port of Sunderland, making it also the most significant urban development in Historic County Durham. (The town was incorporated by the Bishop of Durham in 1634 and had a population of 2,500 by the end of that century.)

Most of the traditional jobs on Wearside were associated with the river or the sea. Shipworkers, dockers, sailors, shipbuilders and fishermen were likely to be close by, as were those who worked in the glass and pottery industries.

Modern County Durham

The modern administrative county of Durham (Modern County Durham) is much smaller than the former County Durham (Historic County Durham), which was a hive of industry in the nineteenth century. Today, many of the industrial and former industrial areas of Historic County Durham lie within the bounds of Tyneside, Wearside and the Tees Valley.

Durham City remains the centre of the county and the bishopric, and boasts a castle, cathedral and county hall. Although the 'Old Durham' site of Durham City dates back to Roman times, it only came into its own towards the end of the Saxon period when a group of monks chose it for the last resting-place of the body of St Cuthbert.

With the Norman Conquest came the construction of the cathedral recognised today as one of the most solid and dramatic in the world. 'Half church of God and half castle' was how Sir Walter Scott described it. A visit to the cathedral confirms the wonder of its positioning – high on a hill bound in by a natural curve in the River Wear and guarded on its vulnerable side by the castle (home today to some of the city's students).

With much of its religious power waning after the dissolution of the monasteries, Durham City was described in the late-sixteenth century as one of

Durham's magnificent cathedral.

shopkeepers with an overlay of religious dignitaries and lawyers. It also had strong links with coalmining and possesses a university with fine traditions and a reputation much in line with that of Oxford and Cambridge. Quite naturally, in a county strong in mining and agriculture, the city also served as a market-town.

In the west of the county lies the former iron-and-steel town of Consett. Some three hundred years ago, German refugees fleeing the Thirty Years War brought expertise in working metal to this area and swordmakers created a local industry here long before Sheffield became famous.

To the south and mid-west of the county are the market-towns of Bishop Auckland and Barnard Castle. The former is the home of the Bishop of Durham; the latter is famed for its rugby-playing school and Bowes Museum, and has links with both Charles Dickens and Oliver Cromwell.

Sedgefield is yet another small market-based community. Centre of the parliamentary constituency of Labour Prime Minister Tony Blair, it is also known for its racecourse.

To the west lie the Durham Dales – Weardale and Teesdale – the latter marking the border of Modern County Durham. Their many villages once populated by miners and agricultural workers, the dales are now popular with walkers and holidaymakers. Here can be found many villages with fine greens and churches; Romaldkirk and Cotherstone in Teesdale are good examples. Wolsingham, Frosterley (famed for its 'marble' or decorative limestone), St John's Chapel and Stanhope are key communities in Weardale.

To the north of Durham City, in the centre of a mining area, lies another market-town, Chester-le-Street. For centuries, it straddled the old Great North Road leading to Newcastle and on to Scotland. It too was the resting-place of the body of St Cuthbert for a short time.

Coastal East Durham encompasses the former colliery communities of Seaham, Easington, Horden and Blackhall. Undersea workings ensured that coalmining continued here late into the twentieth century. The 1984/5 Miners' Strike and its aftermath had important consequences for this part of the county. The successful feature film *Billy Elliot*, based around the declining coal industry, was made in and around Easington.

Newton Aycliffe is the oldest 'new town' in the north of England. Now with a population of 30,000, it was founded under the New Towns Act of 1946 with the intention of improving employment prospects in heavy industrial areas.

The decline in the old industries was also a major reason behind the development of the 'new town' of Peterlee close to the eastern colliery communities. Established in the 1950s and named after a miners' leader, Peterlee housed many workers who had changed occupations as traditional work became less available. Industrial estates sprang up in and around the town with factory space adapted to the newer light industries.

Despite the industrial past of Historic County Durham, its modern counterpart is remarkably rural with large areas of sparsely settled moorland and rough grazing.

Tees Valley

Of all the areas in the North Country that have seen change in terms of organisation and reorganisation, the Tees Valley has probably seen the most. Today this rather vague political entity consists of five major groupings: Hartlepool, Stockton, Darlington, Middlesbrough and the joint authority of Redcar and Cleveland. Included in these are areas formerly in Yorkshire, which feature more heavily in the appropriate volume in this series.

Of those areas in the Tees Valley that were once in Historic County Durham, Hartlepool lies on the coast a few miles north of the mouth of the Tees. Today it is a small unitary authority which covers the former towns of Hartlepool (known locally as 'Old Hartlepool' or The Headland) and West Hartlepool. Before the towns were united under the single banner of Hartlepool in the late-twentieth century, they were commonly referred to as 'The Hartlepools'.

Old Hartlepool has a history stretching back to Saxon times and earlier; West Hartlepool was a nineteenth-century development, based initially on the railways and coal export. Both towns grew as a result of the industrial revolution and benefited from developments in most of the major heavy industries. Part of modern Hartlepool is Seaton Carew – an ancient spa which enjoyed popularity in the inter-war years on account of cheap day railway travel from the local collieries.

Today, Stockton Borough Council embraces the four main settlements of Stockton and Billingham (Historic County Durham) and Yarm and Thornaby (Historic Yorkshire).

Stockton itself is a former market-town on the Tees. In 1310, it was granted the right to hold a market on every Wednesday for ever and was a major river port in the eighteenth century. Pennine lead and farm produce came here overland via horse-and-cart and was then shipped to London and overseas.

Stockton is linked inevitably with the development of the railways as one end of the Stockton and Darlington Railway. Billingham developed into a twentieth-century 'new town' mostly based on the growth of the local chemical industries.

At the other end of the world-famous railway line lay Darlington, yet another market-town and strongly linked to the Quaker movement (see chapter 7, Religion). It is a town of historic importance in more ways than one. By the Middle Ages, it had become a flourishing industrial town, important for the export of wool and for the weaving and dyeing of cloth. In the eighteenth century, its thriving market was at the centre of a local agricultural revolution.

With the coming of the railways, railway and general structural-engineering firms were established, including Darlington Forge, Darlington Railway

Locomotive Works (North Road Shops) and the world-famous Whessoe and Cleveland Bridge (later Kvaerner Cleveland Bridge).

Darlington suffered with the closure of the railway works in the 1960s, and for Stockton and Hartlepool too the late-twentieth century was a period of heavy industrial decline. In all three cases, modern, lighter industries are now the order of the day.

The Tees Valley south of the river lies within the Yorkshire remit. Here, the growth of Middlesbrough, once dubbed 'the fastest-growing town in England' was of great significance. In many ways its story is similar to those of Barrow-in-Furness on the west coast and West Hartlepool to the east. Middlesbrough's development was earlier and more marked than that of the other two and, drawing on the discovery of ironstone in the Cleveland Hills, the town became involved in most aspects of heavy industry.

Further into Yorkshire lies Redcar and Cleveland, described today as 'on the edge of the North York Moors National Park'. The borough contains the significant communities of Redcar, Marske and Saltburn, plus Guisborough, Great Ayton, Skelton, Skinningrove and Kirkleatham, and is one 'rich in industrial heritage'.

While looking into the Tees Valley area, researchers will also come across the terms 'Teesside' and 'Cleveland' which have both, in times past, had official and unofficial roles to play. Unfortunately, even a mere definition of these terms tends to add to the confusion!

Moving On

Thus we have a region with as many individual characteristics as points of common interest, yet these interests are strong enough to make a topic-based study of them viable and useful to the family historian.

The first section is therefore entitled Work in the North Country. Clearly **mining** in its various forms deserves consideration here, as do **shipbuilding, iron manufacture and engineering**. All these, in one way or another, became interlinked.

Agriculture and **transport** have long been 'industries' in themselves, and formed a vital part of working life for many North Country men and women.

There were also **other industries** of significance such as cloth production, fishing and glass-making. As with the 'bigger' industries, they were rarely tied to one specific area.

Next it is feasible to group together features beyond the world of work and classify them under the broad heading North Country Life. Here we can discover the roles of **religion** and **government** in the lives of our ancestors and recognise how both have become great providers of key sources of evidence for the family historian.

Warfare, a candidate perhaps for the Work section, is positioned here as the topic also includes information on the effect of war on the civilian population. Details of **education** can help us appreciate how different early life was for many of our ancestors. The role of **leisure** in North Country life is dealt with in this section too, and some attempt is made to unravel the tangled webs of **dialect** and **diet**.

In both these sections, there are subsections on Finding More and brief guides, where appropriate, to putting Flesh on the Bones by discussing some of the numerous heritage sites and museums operating in the region.

A third section is dedicated to an understanding of the role of **movement**, both into and out of the region and, indeed, around inside it. Such was the restless nature of recorded North Country life that few researchers are fortunate (or perhaps unfortunate) enough to have discovered a complete set of ancestors firmly rooted to one spot! In many ways, reaching an understanding of both how and why ancestors moved can be the most rewarding aspect of genealogical research.

Finally the Research Guide provides handy up-to-date details on the resources necessary for chasing up your North Country ancestors.

Section One

WORK IN THE NORTH COUNTRY

Chapter One

MINING

It is said that at one time you could shout down almost any hole in the world and a Cornishman would pop up. Famed as Cornwall is for mining, the North Country too has much to shout about, and in virtually every area of the industry.

The North is a region known chiefly for its involvement in coal extraction. Coal was collected for centuries from near the surface and, later, taken out of ever-deepening mines in virtually every part of the region.

In Northumberland, the key coal areas lay mostly to the north of Newcastle; on Tyneside there were mines clustered close to both banks of the river. On Wearside, coal was extracted in Sunderland itself and in mining villages such as Hetton-le-Hole, Houghton-le-Spring and Washington.

In Historic County Durham, the early developments tended to be in the west, where the coal was to be found nearer the surface. As time passed, the move was eastwards towards the coast and thence under the sea. In the twentieth century, this move led to the closure of many of the collieries in the west and the movement of workers to the deeper coastal pits around Easington, Horden, Blackhall and Seaham.

Over on the west coast, mines were to be found in and around Workington, Maryport and Whitehaven, a fact celebrated in their local museums today.

Despite the historic importance of coal, it would be foolish to underestimate the significance of the role played by metal mining in the region's economy.

As far back as Roman times, there were searches for silver and lead. Pennine lead was mined in Cumbria and Historic County Durham; copper turned up in different part of the Lake District; iron ore was the making of the Millom, South Tees Valley and Furness areas in the nineteenth century and these are just a few major examples.

Coal Extraction

By the time of the censuses and efficient public records, North Country folk working in coalmines would have had specific tasks to carry out. This was not always the case. Up until the eighteenth century there was little demand for coal and, with a preference shown for either wood or charcoal, the early coalminer would pick up coal where it was easy to find near the surface. Literature of this period tells of folk in the north of England and Scotland simply going to or for the coals 'in the morning'.

As demand for coal slowly began to increase, adit mines and bell pits started to develop. Even here, one described as a 'miner' would still be carrying out general duties. In an adit mine, he or she would simply follow an outcrop of coal into a hillside until the tunnel was no longer considered safe. In a bell pit (so called because the pit was shaped like a bell), a shaft was dropped onto a seam of coal and worked a short distance in both directions. Workers here would be either cutting the coal or winding it up in a corf, or basket, using a windlass.

From the eighteenth century onwards, pits began to develop practices that would still be recognisable in the twentieth century and this created specific jobs that might be credited to an ancestor in written records.

The main job was that of the hewer, who actually got or 'won' the coal at the coalface. From here it was transported to the bottom of the shaft, in the early days being dragged by women, girls or boys; later it was taken by a putter (frequently a young lad) accompanying a Galloway or pit pony.

In the early days, in a development of the bell pit, horses would be used in winding up the coal. Later the windlass was replaced by water power, and water wheels were developed. Finally, steam engines were used and engine-houses built, bringing with them a host of specialised jobs.

The cages, which were suspended on rope and, later, wire rope, carried coal up, and men and ponies up and down. This form of transport involved a number of different jobs including those of banksman at the surface, onsetter down below and the driver as well as various members of a maintenance team.

At the surface, the coal was separated from any stone left with it and the waste taken to the pit heap. In the nineteenth century these were jobs often carried out by women and older boys.

Surface transport then took over (see chapter 5, Transport).

Coalmines were dangerous places. Gas could cause explosion or suffocation, and water was a constant problem. There were attempts at providing safety; in the eighteenth and nineteenth centuries, the term 'fireman' was used for one who used a lighted taper to check and eradicate pockets of gas; young boys were employed as trappers to open and close trap doors and ensure a flow of air. Later this job was tackled with the aid of automated pumps. Water was pumped up to the pit pond, another job tackled by workers in an engine-house.

The introduction of the miner's safety lamp, associated with Cornishman

Davy and North-Easterners Clanny and Stephenson, was another move towards safety.

Prior to the 1840s, there was little if any regulation of labour in the coalmine, and this is often reflected in the youth of some workers recorded in the census of 1841.

After the 1842 Mines Act began to work alongside the Registration Act of 1836, few if any women, girls and younger boys were employed underground; the youngsters also started to receive some form of education. Prior to this, they had gone to work as early as six years of age, according to the Royal Commission that preceded the Act. One teenager, a Nicholas Hudderson, interviewed at Sunderland's Monkwearmouth Colliery, had worked there since he was nine years old and had already suffered an accident, which left him lame. Hudderson also told the commissioners about a group of boys who had died some three or four years before the Act when a rope snapped and both the basket full of coal and the rope had landed on top of them.

Safety and working conditions improved considerably over the years. Pits moved from private hands to public, back to private and ultimately to public once more.

Mechanisation changed pit life dramatically in the second half of the twentieth century, and the role of the coalminer changed with it. Competition from overseas and from other forms of energy eventually sounded the death-knell of the industry.

The search for the exact role played by an ancestor working within this system can be and dependent on luck and the amount of interest expressed by the official originally collecting the information. Some examples serve to show the nature of this problem.

In many records such as parish registers the single word 'miner' or 'collier' was frequently used although 'miner' might be extended, in some cases to 'coalminer'. At census time in 1881, James Laird of Usworth near Washington, aged fifty-five, and his three sons (aged nineteen to twenty-three) were all returned as 'coalminers'.

Elsewhere in Usworth, the family of Mathew Winship, aged fifty-three, has his son John described as a 'coalminer' but Mathew himself as a 'coalminer deputy overman'. His son Mathew, working in the engine-house, is described as a 'brakesman at colliery'.

At nearby Washington, 61-year-old David Swaddle is recorded as a 'colliery heap keeper' and other members of the family as a 'coalminer weighman' and 'colliery mason'. A married son living further up the street is described as an 'engineman (coalmine) driver'.

As ever, there is the luck of the draw, although officials such as deputies, overmen and managers usually had their positions reported, as did those who worked with the static engines.

As to female workers, the last woman underground in Northumberland and Historic County Durham is believed to have worked a few years before the end of the eighteenth century, whereas women were still reported underground in one West Cumberland pit at the time of the 1842 Act.

In fact one of the first protests against female employment underground came as the result of a visit made to the Whitehaven mines by the writer Ayton in 1813. In his book he describes seeing a young girl assisting a horse to drag a line of baskets; the youngster was 'covered with filth, debased and profligate, and uttering some low obscenity as she passed us by'. Later he describes more girls and young women as 'ragged and beastly in their appearance and with a shameless indecency in their behaviour'. All in all, the manner of the girls seemed, to the writer, to give the place 'the character of hell'.

The Coalmining Districts

Coalmines of various sizes existed right across the region. West Cumberland was an important source of coal though often overlooked in favour of its North-Eastern neighbours. Although there were small pockets of coalmining in North Cumbria and the former county of Westmorland in the eighteenth and nineteenth centuries, it was really West Cumberland that carried the banner, with the major coalfield surrounding the towns of Workington, Whitehaven and Maryport. The coalfield itself was physically small and contained in a coastal strip. Pits here included the Wellington Pit, Duke Pit, Jane Pit and Saltom Pit.

Coal was won in the Whitehaven area between the fourteenth and twentieth centuries. The pits that developed here were dangerous due to the gassy nature of the coal, and many lives were lost.

If nineteenth-century reports are to be believed, conditions in some of the West Cumbrian coalmines remained poor for longer than in other areas. In the 1840s practices were found to continue that, as described above, had died out elsewhere.

The Northumberland coalfield north of Newcastle formed an important part of the Great Northern Coalfield, and Ellington Colliery on the Northumberland coast was to survive longer than any other colliery in the region. Other former mining communities in Northumberland include Pegswood, Seaton Delaval, Cramlington and Bedlington.

For many years the miners in the area around Earsdon and Shiremoor performed a seven-man dance with metal mine utensils, which is usually entered into official lists as a 'sword' dance. The 'rapper dance', as it came to be known, attracted the attention of the Duke of Northumberland, for whom the miners were asked to perform on a number of occasions. After appearing before the king at Alnwick Castle, they became the Royal Earsdon Sword Dancers.

Although this information might well have been included in the chapter on leisure, miners traditionally performed the rapper dance at time of economic hardship and specifically to raise money. Other mining villages in

Northumberland and Historic County Durham had rapper sides in the nineteenth and twentieth centuries and have left photographic evidence in archives across the region.

Writers visiting Tyneside have left us fine views of the working conditions for our coalmining ancestors. Fraujas Saint Frond was such a visitor. In 1784 he found a pit with thirty men working above ground and seventy below. In addition there were twenty horses below ground and another four above ground operating the coal-raising machinery. The buckets carrying the coal were made of osier, not wood, had iron handles and could carry 'twelve hundred pounds of coal each'.

Tyneside can also lay claim to a major role in the development of the miner's safety lamp. The Felling Disaster at Gateshead in 1812 cost ninety-two lives, and the names, jobs and ages of the deceased are used frequently as source material in modern school textbooks.

The Society For Preventing Accidents in Coalmines was founded the following year and inventors, including those with North-Eastern connections, began to experiment with the idea of a safety lamp.

Many coalmines on Wearside used the river for transport, and the colliery at Monkwearmouth, now the site of Sunderland AFC's Stadium of Light, lies beside the river and close to the coast. Monkwearmouth was a hot and sulphurous pit and young miners interviewed by the Royal Commission preparing the Mines Act of 1842 painted a fairly bleak picture of life underground there. One teenager said that the smell frequently put him off his food.

Other Wearside pits included Ryhope, Silksworth and Herrington, as well as those in the villages mentioned above. Work on the Hillside cemetery at

Coalminers' homes, West Durham.

Houghton-le-Spring has also brought to light interesting information about local mines and miners (see chapter 7, Religion).

In Historic County Durham, collieries could be found in every corner, and even the modern, more rural county possesses the remnants of numerous mining communities.

In 1842, William Morrison of Chester-le-Street described a typical Durham coalmining colleague to a Royal Commission:

> His stature is diminutive, his figure disproportionate and misshapen; his legs being much bowed, his chest protruding. His countenance is not less striking than his figure; his cheeks being generally hollow, his brow overhanging, his cheekbones high, his forehead low and retreating. Nor is his appearance healthful.

The county also had its share of mining tragedies. Trimdon Grange, Seaham and Easington, all sites of famous pit accidents, still lie within the bounds of Modern County Durham.

A banner still carried at Durham's Big Meeting.

A reminder of the heritage of coal – Modern County Durham.

What is Coal?

An Anthology of Mining Poetry by the Pupils past and present, Staff and Friends of Parkside Infant School, Seaham together with extracts from contemporary works.

The disasters at Trimdon Grange and Seaham both occurred in the nine-teenth century and gave rise to a number of songs and ballads. In the case of Trimdon Grange, the pitman poet Tommy Armstrong mentions victims by name in his song, and Seaham ballads refer to the horrors of entombment and to victims who lived long enough to scribble final messages to their loved ones.

The Easington Disaster occurred within living memory, in 1951, and was the second-biggest disaster in the history of the Durham coalfield. An explosion entombed eighty-one miners, and two rescue workers also died, overcome by poisonous gas. The dead in this case ranged from teenagers to men in their sixties.

The worst disaster in the whole Durham coalfield occurred in 1909 at West Stanley, part of Modern County Durham. Here 168 men died. The deaths came as the result of a single explosion, caused by dust, according to the official enquiry. One of the heroes of the explosion, who was responsible for the rescue of twenty-six men, was Frank Keegan, grandfather of the future England foot-ball star, Kevin Keegan.

*Symbol of a lost industry
– Modern County
Durham.*

Some miners from the west of the county, fondly nicknamed the 'hillbillies', found work in the surviving east-coast pits but the long and often bitter Miners' Strike of the 1980s failed to save the last of these working collieries.

There are no longer coalmines in Modern County Durham although Durham City is still associated with the annual miners' gala, which continues despite the closure of the coalmines and is strongly supported by local heritage groups.

Metal Extraction

Metal mining frequently plays second fiddle to coalmining in history books about the North Country, yet the industry employed huge numbers, certainly up to the end of the nineteenth century. Metal miners found it fairly easy to move from mining one form of metal to mining another within the region (see chapter 14, Movement).

There were ways in which the life of a northern metal miner would have been different from that of a coalminer. There was no gas to contend with, but the metal mines tended to be very damp. Metal miners worked in a cave-like

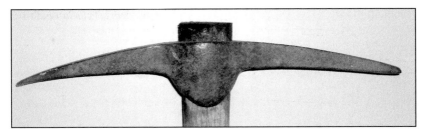

A pick used in the Cumbrian iron mines.

environment rather than working narrow seams as the collier did. They tended to work and be employed in teams and a great deal of time could be taken up with ensuring the safety of movement and working conditions.

As in the coalmines, the engine-houses were important and employed large numbers. Often the job of the engines was to drive pumps to get rid of the water, and for many years and in many places ladders were used rather than cages because of the difficult nature of the underground workings.

The role of women and children in metal mines was traditionally different from that in coalmines. Few if any worked below ground, even before the reforms of the nineteenth century. Instead they worked at the surface separating the ore from the stone, flattening the metal and getting rid of the rock by wheelbarrow. This was preferable to underground work, perhaps, but still a far-from-healthy existence, handling the damp ore and waste.

Ancestors might also be found working in the buildings at the surface in the smiths' shops, powder stores and 'drys', and also in the count house, where the metal was assessed and stamped before being moved on.

As in other mining regions of Britain, the details provided for northern metal miners in official records are dependent on the thoroughness of the clerk. In most cases the simple terms 'miner' or 'underground miner' tend to be used, although frequently the kind of metal – lead, copper or iron – has been helpfully inserted.

As with the coalmines, official records for metal mines tended to be more detailed on those working in positions of responsibility or in the engine-houses. In the Pennine area around Nenthead, for example, many workers in 1851 and 1871 were described as 'lead miners', 'lead ore washers' or 'lead smelters' which does allow for some kind of distinction.

Most workers at Coniston in 1861 were simply put down as 'copper miners'. In the 1881 census of Millom in Cumbria, men at the mine were described as 'iron miners' although in one or two cases they have other jobs too, such as grocer or milkman or even publican.

Thomas Stephens, a Devon-born miner working in Millom, was returned as an 'iron-ore miner' in nearly every public record of his adult life. His father-in-law, John Bunny, was more helpfully described at various times as an 'underground haulage driver', an 'engine driver 'and, ultimately, as the 'driver of a stationary engine'.

All mining communities had their share of blacksmiths although, sadly, it is sometimes difficult to work out if all were actually employed in the mining industry. We should be thankful to census enumerators who bothered to label certain workers as 'blacksmith miners' and 'blacksmith apprentices in the mines'. If only more enumerators had taken the time to be so helpfully descriptive!

With the closure of metal mines from the nineteenth century onwards, a great deal of movement took place and it is likely that few descendants of these men and women now live in the area.

The Metal Mining Districts

During the heyday of metal mining in the nineteenth century, metal mines could be found all across the region. The Pennine area was particularly busy, with over forty mines in Teesdale and over thirty in Weardale in the early-nineteenth century, plus those in the Derwent Valley and spilling over the top into Cumbria too.

In Cumbria there were iron-ore mines and copper mines in and around the south-western fringes of the Lake District. There were also silver and lead on the eastern fringes of the lakes around Caldbeck. From there it was across to the lead, silver and zinc mines of the Cumbrian Pennines.

Lead and copper in particular were mined around Keswick and Coniston, near Ullswater and in the Skiddaw area.

Iron ore was mined at Cleator Moor in West Cumberland from the 1840s to the early-twentieth century. Here there existed a community almost entirely composed of iron-ore miners. Egremont and Lindal-in-Furness also boasted iron-ore mines, and the Hodbarrow Mine at Millom was renowned for its fine Cornish beam-engines and constant efforts to keep the sea away from the mine workings.

In lead mining alone, one commentator noted that by the end of the eighteenth century the Weardale, Teesdale, Allendale and Alston areas formed 'an important element in the country's economy'. A visitor to Teesdale in 1848 gave a brief description of the lives of local lead miners:

> They stay here for about five months in the year, dig out the lead ore, break it up with hammers into small pieces, then wash it and carry it for a short way in bags to where there is a track for donkeys or ponies to travel on.

Many of these mines failed to survive the nineteenth century, destroyed by overseas competition, with the price of English lead almost halving between 1877 and 1885.

The later discovery of iron in the Furness area around Dalton and in Millom opened new avenues. The iron mines were to survive into the twentieth century but not the twenty-first.

The metal mines were responsible for a great deal of movement. Millom in West Cumbria, for example, was heaving with folk from Devon and Cornwall. For some time after moving, former South-Westerner continued to marry former South-Westerner too (see chapter 14, Movement).

The same applied to the mining settlement at Roose near Barrow-in-Furness. In 1881 three-quarters of the families there had origins in Cornwall and Devon, and names common to the South-West, such as Rickard from Breage, Trembath from Ludgvan and Richards could be found.

There was also considerable movement within Cumbria, with miners heading to Millom in the late-nineteenth century from declining lead and copper mines elsewhere in the county.

In the Tees Valley area, the metal industry was dependent on the ore mined in the Cleveland Hills (which lie outside the region covered by this book).

Green slate was also mined around Kentmere and Longsleddale on the eastern fringes of Lakeland, and graphite, plumbago or 'wadd' was mined in Borrowdale and used in pencil manufacture. There were also important slate quarries around the Honister and Coniston area.

Finding More

Documents relevant to the history of mining and potentially useful to the family historian can be seen in most of the region's major archive centres. Some of these resources are regional, such as Royal Commissions, committee and inspection reports. In the case of Royal Commissions, individual miners were often interviewed and accounts of those interviews published.

The Cumbria Archives at Whitehaven and Barrow both possess mining records. In the case of the Whitehaven office, these cover coal, metal and slate as well as the activities of the National Union of Miners.

Some material relating to viewers' reports on West Cumbrian coalmines can also be found in the Tyne and Wear Archives at Newcastle.

The Barrow office has material relating to both the Hodbarrow Iron Mine at Millom and the papers of the Duke of Buccleuch.

Details of many of the mining-related documents available at the new Northumberland archives can be viewed on their electronic catalogue. There are photographs and postcards connected to coalmining, particularly in the twentieth century, and many other relevant documents.

These include the details of the 1762 sale of a coalmine on Anick Common, the property of Edward Errington, and records of colliery companies. Material pertaining to the Northumberland Miners' Mutual Confident Association and the Cowpen miners' lodges seem to be particularly extensive here. One or two items also relate to the metal mines in the far south-west of the county.

The Tyne and Wear Archives has mining material relevant to the North-East, Northumberland, Tyneside, Modern County Durham and Wearside. These include individual viewers' reports for Washington and Wearmouth on Wearside and Felling on Tyneside. There are also occasional gems such as the will of George Stoker, offputter at Benwell Colliery on Tyneside in 1841.

Records for the Northumberland and Durham Miners' Permanent Relief Fund Friendly Society also exist from the mid-nineteenth century; applicants registers are also kept here.

The Durham County Record Office has accessible information on individual collieries and the office has material relating to colliery companies and the National Coal Board pre-nationalisation. Information on these can be accessed on its website.

The same website also gives access to the informative Durham Collieries site, which covers collieries in Historic County Durham from the middle of the nineteenth century to the end of the twentieth century. Information on the site has been gathered from many sources and can be accessed through names, townships and maps. This site also has a useful 'Help Page'.

County Durham Libraries are also involved in a number of mining-related projects useful to students of family history. These include the Durham Miner Project, which has been responsible for recording and presenting the working, social and environmental sides of County Durham's mining history (coal and lead).

The Coal Mining Oral History Project has also tapped into important resources by recording the memories of people who lived and worked in the mining villages of County Durham.

Some interesting material remains in private hands. For example, work is currently going on on the journals of Mark Swaddle, who controlled a pit engine at Washington during the late part of the nineteenth century. Swaddle was a deeply religious man and a confirmed trade unionist. He represented his colleagues at a number of important meetings about pay and conditions. His journals, which cover daily life in Washington, pit accidents, strikers and attitudes to what was happening in the wider world, are real treasures (the original diaries remain with his descendants).

Details of miners from the Far North and their working and social lives also turn up in documents forming part of nation-wide surveys and reports; these can be viewed at important national resource centres such as The National Archives.

Flesh on the Bones

The importance of mining in the North Country is reflected in the number of museums and museum galleries dedicated to the social and working life of miners.

In Cumbria, the Helena Thompson Museum at Workington deals with all aspects of local history including coalmining; the Florence Mine Heritage Centre nearby specialises in minerals and claims rights as the last deep working iron-ore mine in western Europe.

Nearby at Whitehaven, the Haig Colliery Museum is making rapid advances due to grants and has concentrated on the restoration of the pit's winding engine and engine-house.

Millom has long boasted a friendly and successful folk museum, which has been revamped recently. Here can be seen a reconstruction of iron-ore mine workings incorporating a cage, artefacts connected with Millom ironworks, and the interior of a miner's cottage.

Metal mining is also celebrated in the east of the county at the Nenthead Mines Heritage Centre near Alston. The main metals mined here were lead, silver and zinc and there are displays featuring water power.

The centre also runs underground tours through 'England's highest and largest lead mining complex' and provides an opportunity for panning like a prospector. The mine buildings have been restored to give a feel for work and life in the nineteenth century.

The Honister Slate Museum on Fleetwith Pike between Buttermere and Borrowdale cover the history of slate mining. This mining complex was 'hacked out by Victorian miners with handtools by candlelight' and the museum shows the hardship the work entailed.

The Pencil Museum in Keswick claims to be the only one of its type in the world and will be of interest to those whose ancestors were involved in the mining of Borrowdale graphite. The separate Keswick museum also deals with the town's mining history.

The Colliery Museum at Woodhorn near Ashington in Northumberland is just starting a new lease of life as part of a modern complex, which embraces the new Northumberland Archives. The museum is based in the original colliery and has a large number of exhibits recording the social and mining history in the area.

The remodelling of Woodhorn has taken well over two years and the museum stands as an important resource for the lives of anyone involved in the coal industry in Northumberland.

One of the main features of the new Woodhorn is 'Coal Town' – an interactive insight into all aspects of working and social life in Ashington in the twentieth century.

Bellingham Heritage Centre deals specifically with the history of the North Tyne and Redesdale area, and features mining displays.

On Tyneside, Wallsend's Segedunum Museum displays artefacts connected to coalmining, including safety lamps and tools, and features the history of Wallsend Colliery, which was one of the world's most productive pits between the 1780s and the 1850s.

Newcastle's Discovery Museum has a number of displays relevant to the working and social lives of Tyneside miners.

On Wearside, Sunderland Museum and Winter Gardens has a gallery dedicated to coalmining with some material from the Seaham Colliery Disaster of 1881 (although Seaham itself is in Modern County Durham). The display includes some of the moving messages left behind by the victims.

F Pit Museum at Washington is open only at specific times from spring to autumn. The museum is housed in the engine-house of the former colliery, which closed in the 1960s.

The museum will be of particular interest to those whose ancestors were involved in the transport of coal from the bottom of the pit shaft to the top. Upstairs there is an engine that was constructed in the late-nineteenth century. It is still in working order, though now operated at a slightly slower speed than it was during its working life.

There is also a model of the pit and the area around it as it was in the middle of the twentieth century and displays showing the history of coal-winding from human muscle power through horse and water wheel to steam.

Examples of the local context can be found in and around the twentieth-century colliery village at Beamish Museum in Modern County Durham. Here there is a stone engine-house containing the impressive Steam Winder which was built in 1855 by J and G Joicey and Co. for Beamish Colliery 2nd Pit.

The Drift Mine at Beamish was originally opened in the middle of the nineteenth century. The mine was closed in 1958 but has been partly reopened to allow visitors to experience life in this form of pit.

The North of England Lead Mining Museum at Killhope recalls the days when the Durham dales and the surrounding areas of Cumbria formed the bustling heart of the world's lead mining industry.

Killhope was just one of many metal mines scattered through the area and has enjoyed extensive restoration in recent years. The museum offers hands-on experience and is known for its working water wheel. The mine itself lies 450 metres above sea level and visitors can find out about both the working and home lives of the miners and methods of finding and washing the lead ore.

In the former Yorkshire area of the Tees Valley, a mining museum on the site of Loftus Mine recalls the days when this was one of the most important sources of British iron.

Chapter Two

SHIPBUILDING

Shipbuilding was an important industry on both coasts of the region, where workers became involved in the production of vessels of all shapes and sizes and constructed for many different purposes.

On the east coast there were yards all along the lower reaches of the Tyne, and at Sunderland, Hartlepool, Stockton and Middlesbrough. The yards on the Tyne specialised in warships, large-tonnage passenger vessels, cargo liners and food ships. Those on the Wear, because it is a narrow river, generally built medium-sized tramp steamers and colliers. The yards further south, in the Hartlepools and around the Tees, followed the Wear pattern.

On the west coast, shipbuilding flourished in Barrow-in-Furness and further up the coast at Whitehaven and Maryport. Indeed, Whitehaven was one of the most successful of early shipbuilding bases, with effective shipbuilding taking place in the eighteenth century. Maryport's shipbuilding industry developed and prospered alongside the general growth of the town. The yards at Barrow-in-Furness, developed from the nineteenth century onwards, produced all different kinds of vessel, from passenger ships to naval ships and submarines.

Ship repair too was an important occupation in the region, and the patterns of repair undertaken differed from port to port. The dry-dock at Hebburn, for example, was renowned in the early-twentieth century for its refitting.

The shipyards brought with them many other forms of related work. After the development of the steamship in the early and middle parts of the nineteenth century, marine engineering became very important, developing in or close to the shipyards. Sunderland was also known for its anchor production, and it is fitting that a Sunderland-made anchor proudly stands outside the main door of the National Maritime Museum at Greenwich.

Statistics exist in abundance, many pointing to the importance of the North-East yards in particular. In 1901, when just over half of the world's ships were constructed in Britain, more than fifty per cent of these were built on that coast. Just before the First World War, half of the UK's production of ships, and more than half of its repair business, still lay in the North-East. When these figures

Sunderland-built anchor outside the National Maritime Museum.

are added to the production figures for the west coast, they clearly pinpoint the importance of the industry in the lives of North Country ancestors.

Sail and Steam

Although there is some evidence for shipbuilding in the region during medieval times, the great days of the building of sailing ships for the whole region are actually dateable to the early-nineteenth century.

In a magnificent work on the sailing ships of the Tyne, Richard Keys chronicles the whole period from 1830 to 1930. He notes that, of the sailing ships owned or registered on the Tyne during this period, twenty-five per cent were built on Tyneside, thirty-five per cent on the Wear, twenty-three per cent at other places in the United Kingdom, eleven per cent in Canada and three per cent in the USA.

This variety can be confirmed by examining the career of any long-serving sailing captain in the North-East during this period. Between 1858 and 1865, for example, Captain George Pottinger of South Shields, who worked out of the Tyne, captained ships built in Dumbarton, Shields and New Brunswick.

The sailing ships varied in shape and size, and even in name. Keys talks about 'contentious classification' of sailing ships, with at least ten names used in the description of Tyneside vessels. The most common type of vessel used for trading here was the three-masted barque. The queen of the seas was the clipper, or full-rigged ship, which had three masts all bearing square-rigged sails. There were also a series of small two-masters known as 'snows'. The last fully rigged composite (iron frame and wooden hull) passenger clipper, the *Torrens*, was constructed in Sunderland.

The yards producing sailing ships had their own special suppliers, the most important of which were providers of timber and the manufacturers of rope, sails and appropriate metalwork for use in and around the wooden vessels.

The beginning of the steamship age in the North is dateable. Palmer's yard, on the south bank of the Tyne at Jarrow, the brainchild of Mark and George Palmer, produced the screw-propelled iron collier *John Bowes* in 1852, thus beginning the age of the coastal collier steamer. Change had been made necessary by the success of the railways, which developed rapidly during the 1830s and 1840s. Although the train was both quicker and cheaper than the wooden-walled sea vessel, the iron steamer was able to put up a real challenge.

Researchers into shipbuilding ancestry may be lucky enough to find ancestors described in some documents as more than mere labourers or 'shipyard workers'. Shipwrights, caulkers, riveters, platers, welders and patternmakers were all involved in ship construction. Platers had assistants, whom they hired and fired personally. There were also various types of smiths and painters supported by the likes of rivetmakers and wire ropemakers.

Whereas shipwrights constructed wooden ships, the coming of metal vessels (iron and, later, steel) brought specialist jobs. They saw the birth of the 'black squads'; the boilermakers often drawn out of the iron industry, like the Hughes family, who moved from Dudley in the Black Country to Barrow-in-Furness.

Others were drawn in from older industries. George Gregson (born in Preston in 1870) moved to Barrow with his father, who had been a cottonmill operative. By the 1880s George was an apprentice boilersmith in the shipyards. In later official documents, he is registered as a boilermaker.

In the 1871 census for Willington on Tyneside, Stephenson Street had an engineer in a dredger, three shipyard labourers and a shipwright living close by each other.

For the shipyard workers, the work was physical and the hours long. Theirs was not generally considered to be a well-paid occupation. The likes of boilermakers were often paid piecework, while the shipwrights were paid for timed work. It was thus possible to have a 'boilermaker journeyman'.

As in many of the factories of the industrial revolution, there was strict regulation. Work usually started at 6 am and a lock-out for late arrival could cost a quarter of a day's pay, with poor weather, as in the winter months, bringing no pay at all.

Shipbuilding in the nineteenth century was a tough way of life with little in the way of compensation for accident or injury. Yet, as in the coalmines, the shipyards tended to look after their own and family members were often found jobs. Even in the twentieth century, a son might be found an apprenticeship after an accident had cost a father his job or even his life. After the Second World War there was some improvement in safety measures.

Ship ownership and shipbuilding were closely linked. In the nineteenth century, a ship could be divided up into sixty-four lots, which could be owned by a single company or by a group of individuals. Caution is needed here in ancestral research, as someone described in official documents as a 'shipowner' might, in truth, be the owner of a sixty-fourth of a very tiny vessel.

Shipowners were often merchants, shipbuilders and master mariners. Others involved were ship chandlers, shipbrokers, sailmakers, ropemakers, wharfingers and anchor and chain manufacturers. These too are all terms that might turn up in a census or other documentation.

One good example of a North-Eastern shipowner is Henry Milvain, who lived at North Elswick Hall in Newcastle. Scottish by birth, he was originally in the drapery business and became sole owner of seventeen of the best sailing vessels on the Tyne in the mid-nineteenth century. Another example is Scottish-born Northumbrian Walter Runciman, who started life as a master mariner then became a shipowner and famous politician and writer.

Marine engineering was important enough to shipbuilding from the 1850s onwards to merit a place here. It was one of several branches of engineering to flourish in the region (see chapter 6, Other Industries). On Wearside, marine engineering developed from the 1820s, and most yards had their own engine works.

Parsons, in particular, gained world-wide fame for engineering.

Shipowners' houses in Sunderland.

The Shipbuilding Communities

As previously mentioned, communities were heavily dependent on ship-building for their existence on both the west coast and the east.

Whitehaven in the west was one of the most successful of the early ship-building places, with shipbuilding taking place in the eighteenth century at the yard of Daniel Brocklebank. The Brocklebank family continued its links with the town when later working out of Liverpool. The Whitehaven Shipbuilding Company enjoyed later success but then experienced difficulty in launching larger vessels, and this eventually spelt the end of a once thriving industry.

The Maryport experience is an interesting one. Although fishing vessels had been built in the area prior to this date, it was in the latter part of the eighteenth century that shipbuilding really took off in the port under the auspices of John Bell.

The River Ellen, on which Maryport stands, is narrow, which necessitated broadside launches from the mid-nineteenth century onwards. Soon after, the Ritsons, who built the vessels, and the Monkhouses, who rigged them, dominated the industry.

Maryport continued to enjoy success into the age of the steamship but was eventually brought down in the early-twentieth century by lack of support industries. Steamships had to be towed to either the Clyde or the Tyne to have their boilers and engines installed. With fierce competition from those ship-builders who had this facility on site, shipbuilding on the Ellen began to prove uneconomic.

The Barrow docks were opened in 1867 and, by the 1890s, the Barrow Shipbuilding Company had turned into the world-famous Vickers organisation. In addition to well-known liners, Vickers produced many illustrious naval ships and submarines from the first Royal Navy submarine in 1901 to the nuclear submarines of the late-twentieth century.

The Tyne too had a reputation for constructing ships of all kinds: the legendary passenger ship *Mauretania* was launched here in 1906. Shipbuilders also had a special eye to naval construction, a trade that was linked to armaments works further upstream.

Swan Hunter set up at Wallsend in the 1860s and its naval yard at Walker was working until the late-twentieth century. The *Resolution* was built on the Tyne in 1892, the destroyer *Scourge* in 1910 and the cruiser *Manchester* in 1937.

Armstrong's factory, featured in the song 'The Blaydon Races', started at Elswick in 1847 with cranes and later began the production of armaments before moving beyond the bridges and closer to river-mouth in 1912.

The steam turbine was also developed on Tyneside, providing the power essential to our modern lifestyle. It was the brainchild of Charles Parsons, created in the 1880s for the purpose of producing electricity. His work eventually led to the construction of the *Turbinia*, the world's first steam-turbine-driven vessel. This in turn enabled the construction of faster warships, passenger liners and cargo ships.

With a common interest in naval construction, both Tyneside and Barrow became involved in contracts with foreign navies, which in turn led to visits from navies from the Far East. These visits aroused great public interest, frequently led to family days out and are often mentioned in diaries and songs of the period.

When Chinese sailors came to take over a ship in Newcastle in 1881, a local songwriter came up with the following chorus:

> *John Chinaman, John Chinaman*
> *What have you come to see?*
> *What do you think of our town, lads?*
> *How do you like our quay?*

On Wearside, it was natural that shipbuilding should develop as a major industry alongside the growth and expansion of the port. This development, matching others elsewhere in the North Country, is worth considering in some detail.

Ships were built in the area since medieval times, yet it was not until the nineteenth century that the town really started to forge a reputation, both for its shipbuilding and repairing.

No further praise can be heaped on Sunderland than that of a Tyneside rival,

Old shipbuilding cranes on Tyneside.

Swan Hunter's shipbuilding yard on Tyneside.

Victorian songwriter Joe Wilson. He wrote this song (transcribed from dialect) specifically for a professional performance in the town in the mid-nineteenth century:

> *What a great success they've made*
> *In most every kind of trade*
> *No shipbuilders in the world they'll ever fear*
> *And great launches keep their pride*
> *Always on the brightest side*
> *And the sailors all declare so on the Wear*

As early as 1819, when wooden ships were being built, the Wearside shipbuilding business was reported as standing 'the highest of any in the kingdom'. By the 1830s, Lloyds Register of Shipping marked down Sunderland as 'probably the top shipbuilding town' in the kingdom. Rivers such as the Clyde and the Tyne produced more tonnage in total, yet they relied for their figures on the amalgamation of output of a number of shipbuilding towns.

Between the early-nineteenth century and the production of the last ship in the late-twentieth century, yards of all shapes and sizes developed along the banks of the Wear. Many of them, such as Doxford, Thompson, Austin,

A view of old Sunderland.

Pickersgill, Bartram, Laing and Short were to become household names beyond the boundaries of the port. These were the employers of many a Wearside ancestor.

Doxford's began shipbuilding some miles upstream at Cox Green in 1840 but later moved further down the river to Pallion. This yard was to gain the blue riband for production twice in the early-twentieth century.

Thompson's started on the North Sands in the 1840s and went through various yards and brothers. The company was still going strong in the 1960s and 1970s but was mothballed for some time until it built the giant crane ship *Challenger* in 1986.

Austin's started with wooden collier brigs on the north side of the river in 1826. From 1846 onwards, the business operated on the south side near the main bridge. It suffered badly in the depression and merged with Pickersgill's in 1954. Although its life span was short, Austin Pickersgill was a well-known name in post-war Britain.

Bartram's was based upstream at Hylton in the early-nineteenth century but later moved to the South Dock, where it became the only yard in the country to launch its vessels directly into the sea. In 1968, the firm was taken over by Austin Pickersgill.

The shipbuilder James Laing was born in his father's shipyard at Deptford on the Wear in 1823. He was knighted in 1897. The most famous ship from the yard was the *Torrens*. Launched in 1875, she broke the record for a journey to Adelaide, which was made in sixty-four days. At one point her second mate was the author Joseph Conrad. Laing's last ship was launched in 1985.

Short's was a true family firm. It originally constructed vessels at Hylton but later moved near to the Old Hall at Pallion. The company closed in 1964.

There were other, smaller yards too, such as William Pile and Hay and Company, which launched the *City of Adelaide* in 1864, one of the fastest ocean-going clippers of the time.

Shipbuilding was the lifeblood of Wearside and eventually led to the use of the controversial term 'Mackems' for Wearsiders. Although the origins and first use of the word is much argued about, there is little doubt that it arose from the 'Macking'(making) and 'tacking' (taking) to sea of ships, the whole phrase being originally 'mackem and tackem'.

The shipbuilding achievements of the twin towns of Hartlepool and West Hartlepool are sometimes overlooked due to the success of the Tyne and Wear and also because of the local importance of other industries, such as metal manufacture, timber import and coal export.

In the latter part of the nineteenth century and early part of the twentieth century, West Hartlepool was an important shipbuilding town. Between 1880 and 1914, the West Hartlepool yard of Denton, Gray and William Gray won the blue riband for maximum output of shipping on six occasions.

The firm's Central Marine Engineering Works and Central Shipyard lay at the heart of the dock complex and in 1888 produced and engined a record twenty-two ships of average 3,000 tons.

By 1900, shipbuilding and marine engineering involved almost twenty per cent of the male population of West Hartlepool, though the local industry had its difficulties. As early as 1865, the West Hartlepool shipyard of Pile and Spence collapsed, and a depression in the mid-1880s saw the closure of several small shipyards and engineering works.

As on the west coast, shipbuilding on the Tees really took off in the late-eighteenth century, with ships built at Stockton seeing service in the Napoleonic Wars. Ships were built in Middlesbrough from the early-nineteenth century and the Tees continued to thrive through the age of the screw steamer and steel ship.

Successful firms here included the South Stockton Iron Shipbuilding Company and Pease and Partners. By the end of the nineteenth century, the Tees alone was making a highly significant contribution to the North Country's domination of the world's merchant navy shipbuilding market. This was to continue into the twentieth century with the creation of Smith's Dock just before the First World War.

Most people think of the decline of shipbuilding as specific to certain points in the twentieth century but the history of shipbuilding is punctuated with cycles of growth and recession, which makes generalisation difficult. In the nineteenth century, there were significant slumps in the mid-1880s, and in the twentieth century between 1908 and 1910 and during the 1920s, when some Wearside yards produced nothing at all.

The 1930s were infamous, not least for the hardship of Jarrow, whose un-employed marched to London in protest. In January 1933 almost eighty per cent of male insured workers were unemployed in the town. In the same year only a few thousand gross tons were launched in the North-East overall and, during the inter-war depression, more than twenty yards in the North-East ceased to function. Palmer's yard in modern South Tyneside closed in 1934 and gradually marine engineering began to close down on the Tyne and Wear as well as in the Hartlepools and the area around the Tees.

War, as ever, brought some benefits. Austin's of Sunderland, for example, specialised in constructing coastal vessels to replace those sunk by enemy action, and also built the frigate *Amberley Castle* and some landing craft. During the Second World War twenty-five per cent of the British tonnage produced came from Sunderland.

Even the post-war years are not clear-cut. In the Historic County of Durham (Sunderland, Middlesbrough and the Hartlepools), order books were often full but the main concern was the ability to find enough steel. On Wearside alone, success continued immediately post-war, with the river seeing three launches in a single hour on 6 March 1947.

Economists writing in the 1970s were not totally despondent, though they were aware that continuity of employment was not to be 'easily achieved'. They had spotted Japanese competition but not that from China and Korea. On Wearside there was a brief flourish through links with Greek owners but downsizing and rationalisation was the name of the game, eventually leading to the single Sunderland Shipbuilders, nationalisation and, ultimately, closure. The last Sunderland-made vessel came out of Doxford's in November 1988.

The slumps in shipbuilding, occurring as they did on a fairly regular basis, were often reasons for migration out of the region and the creation of new family units outside the area but still deeply conscious of their North-Eastern heritage (see chapter 14, Movement).

Finding More

A number of records relating to shipbuilding exist in North Country repositories. Cumbrian sources for shipbuilding include the records of the Curwen family of Workington Hall at the Whitehaven Record Office, of Vickers at the Barrow office and of the Lowther family of Whitehaven at the Carlisle office.

As might be expected, the material involving shipbuilding on Tyneside and Wearside is substantial and the main place to find it is at the Tyne and Wear Archives in Newcastle. Some of the mass of material handed over at the closure of the yards remains as yet unsorted. Here, there is material relating to the work of Armstrong's on the Tyne in its various guises (back in some cases to the middle of the nineteenth century), with some records dealing with naval construction.

There are other records of household names in both building and engineering – Swan Hunter, Palmer's of Jarrow, Hawthorn Leslie, Clark Chapman and Parsons among them. Many of the key Wearside shipbuilding records are here too. They relate mostly to activity in the twentieth century but include nineteenth-century material as well.

On the list are records relating to Thompson's, Short Brothers, Doxford's and Laing's.

There are registers of ships and fishing boats for Sunderland and records of organisations connected with the sea – including sailmakers' records back to the seventeenth century.

The Tyne and Wear Archives also has records affecting Hartlepool, with minutes of meetings of the Tyne Wear Tees and Hartlepool Shipbuilders' Associations from 1885 into the early-twentieth century. The archive currently has a handy guide relating to shipbuilding, outfitting, registration and repair.

The construction of some of these iron vessels built on Tyne and Wear can be followed from yard books, many of which still exist and can be found in the Tyne and Wear Archives. These can be of particular interest to researchers with either shipbuilding or maritime ancestry.

Take, for example, the *Efficient*, later to be captained by a brother of Captain George Pottinger, mentioned previously. The *Efficient* was built in Sunderland over the winter of 1876/7. The total cost was just over £25,000 and detailed records of outgoings give some idea of what was involved. Wages were always a big outlay, especially towards the end of production, when time was of the essence and the work very labour-intensive. In the early months of construction, most of the financial outlay was on angle iron, rivets (which were used until the Second World War then later replaced by welding) and timber. Local firms were often the providers here. Later, money went on pitch, tar and paint, pipes, ropes, and, finally, upholstery.

More often than not the actual fitting took place at a different location from the initial construction and launch. The cost of the pair of engines for the *Efficient* came to just under £7,000. This was almost one-third of the total ship cost and gives some clue as to the importance of engineering in the age of the steamship.

Despite the advance of steam, the days of sail lasted much longer than is often assumed. Sail and steam went side-by-side well into the twentieth century, with many vessels able to travel by both methods.

On Wearside itself, the Local Studies Centre at Sunderland has a number of useful collections relating to shipbuilding.

The Corder manuscripts, a unique handwritten collection of thirty-eight complete volumes relating to local topography and family history, include quite extensive material on shipbuilding families.

Pamphlets and posters from the eighteenth and nineteenth centuries are also useful, as are a couple of guides to the history of shipbuilding on the Wear and books concerning the topic.

The Teesside Archives contain a number of interesting records including some relating to the Boilermakers' Society in the twentieth century, Smith's Dock Company from 1890 and Haverton Hill Shipyard from 1898.

Flesh on the Bones

As with mining, there are numerous museums and heritage centres in the region, which feature the story of shipbuilding, although not so many dedicated solely to the industry.

In West Cumbria, the various museums at Workington, Whitehaven and Maryport feature shipbuilding alongside shipping and other important trades and industries. The Maritime Museum at Maryport has a particularly interesting collection, which is well supported on the Internet.

The Helena Thompson Museum at Workington displays shipwrights' tools and wooden half-models, which were used as templates for building ships.

The Dock Museum, Barrow-in-Furness, straddles a Victorian graving dock, and features shipbuilding heavily as part of the town's maritime heritage.

The Segedunum Museum at Wallsend on Tyneside somewhat belies its Latin title. The museum is built on the site of a shipyard and features displays on the shipbuilding industry, for which Wallsend became known across the world. The shipbuilding display details the history of Swan Hunter and the firm's impact. There are models of ships built in the yard, including the *Carpathia*, and computer-generated walks on the *Mauretania*.

The 'Story of the Tyne' forms a major gallery at Newcastle's Discovery Museum and is a must for anyone with ancestors who worked in the Tyneside shipyards. There are many ship and yard models and a large wall map giving details of the organisation of shipbuilding along the river.

A clever exhibition in Newcastle's Discovery Museum's Story of the Tyne Gallery records the nature of naval work on Tyneside. Guns were produced at Elswick, turbines and boilers also north of the river; rope, capstans and paint to the south, and steel further towards the sea at Hebburn.

The Working Lives Gallery at Discovery also features the building of the *Mauretania*, and Parsons's famous *Turbinia*, the first ship powered by steam turbines and, in 1897, the fastest ship in the world, dwarfs the entrance gallery.

The Sunderland Museum and Art Gallery has an entire gallery dedicated to shipbuilding on the Wear. As in the Discovery, there are many models and much material relating to specific yards.

The Museum of Hartlepool is situated in the old dock area and also has displays on shipbuilding in the twin towns of Hartlepool and West Hartlepool. Here too is a Hartlepool-built restored paddle steamer – the *Wingfield Castle* – from the 1930s.

Chapter Three

AGRICULTURE

The phrase 'The Industrial North' has a lot to answer for and disguises the fact that huge swathes of the region were, and still are, essentially rural. The conurbations of Wearside and Tyneside retain a few farms within their boundaries; Modern County Durham and the Tees Valley have large rural areas and both Cumbria and Northumberland remain essentially rural.

The geography of the region has much to do with the history and nature of North Country agriculture. The Saxon settlements on the plains and those of the Vikings on the hills are reflected in the place names and also in the type of farming – sheep in the Pennines, Cheviots and Lakeland, and cattle and arable farming where practicable on lower lands.

A description of the agricultural economy around Durham in the seventeenth century provides a good idea of the way things worked, in one part of the region at least. Here there were wealthy farmers who owned their farms and were described as 'gentlemen' or 'yeomen'. They also rented church lands, farmed several hundred acres and supplied grain and meat to those working in the coal-bearing areas. Beneath these economically were the substantial tenants farming a hundred acres or possibly more. Next came the husbandmen in charge of small family farms and then the small householders with a few acres. By this time, the Open Field system had come to an end in Historic County Durham.

Elsewhere in the region there were many different types of farms, from the large estates found in Northumberland, Durham and Cumbria to the tenant farmers operating under leases, either long or short term.

Letters from farmers working land belonging to the Vane estate on the fringes of the Lake District in the nineteenth century give a good account what life was like for the tenant farmer.

John Richardson, the Vanes' land agent, lived at Hutton just outside Penrith. His time was spent in buying, selling and improving cattle and sheep on Vane lands but also in correspondence with tenants about maintenance and upkeep of property. One note written to him in 1875 refers to a change in tenancy. It came to Richardson from Thomas Noble of Roughtonbeck and reads:

Mr Hinks has had a very good sale indead [sic] and Mr Crosthwaite and him has got all settled up crop and all and Mr Hinks gos [sic] out today at 12 o clock and Mr Crosthwaite enters on Friday.

The farmers (both owners and tenants) employed the majority of those working on the land. These workers were referred to by a variety of names. The common term 'agricultural labourer' or 'ag lab' was most frequently used in documentation, especially as the period of the census opened up; other terms include the wider 'husbandman' and the more upmarket 'yeoman' and 'farmer'. In some cases, those of middling authority might be described as 'farm bailiffs'. There were also specialist shepherds or cowmen and cartmen.

The role of women in agriculture in the region was an important one. In some exceptional early-twentieth-century research carried out by Ivy Pinchbeck, it was noted that in relatively thinly populated places such as Durham, women did much of the work, including haymaking and pea and bean setting. They could often earn 2s 6d a week, which was £12 a year and as much as their male equivalent was making in Cumberland.

In Historic County Durham in the late-eighteenth century, women were more likely to be found in agriculture than in spinning. The writer concludes that the general lack of male hands in both Northumberland and Durham led to more agricultural work for women than in most places in the country.

Interesting changes in agriculture began about the time of the first 'real' census and the beginning of civil registration in England, around 1840. When competition with other farming nations was opened up in 1846 by the scrapping of the infamous Corn Laws, many thought it would be the end of British farming. For a number of reasons – improved methods of agriculture, better research and continental wars – this did not prove to be the case. Instead, Britain entered a Golden Age of Agriculture, which lasted, in some areas, up to 1880.

This development is reflected in the jottings of Joseph Liddell, an agricultural merchant hailing from rural Durham but operating from an office opposite Newcastle Central Station. Three of his business diaries (1869, 1873 and 1880) turned up at a Northumbrian jumble sale and they give an excellent overview of agricultural life in the North Country in the late-nineteenth century. His diary for the 1860s reflects success, with machines, equipment and grasses all up for sale and well sold.

The growth of the railways was particularly important here and many entries show agricultural goods being carried to long-defunct local stations and included such wondrous machines as Ashby and Jeffrey's Celebrated Double Action Haymaker and Hornsby's Champion Ploughs.

The diaries also indicate where agricultural trading took place – at the shows, fairs and markets – and give numerous examples. In his 1869 diary, Liddell notes that he attended Durham Fair and Stallion Show, Durham Agricultural Show, the South Durham Show, the North Yorkshire Horse and Dog Show at Darlington and the Northumberland Agricultural Society Show at Hexham.

There were also ploughing matches held all over the region, with salesmen interested in the performance of their star products. In January 1869, for example, Liddell attended a ploughing match at Mr James's farm at Rudchester organised by the Northumberland Agricultural Society and noted the results in his journal.

Towards the end of the nineteenth century and in the years leading up to the First World War, things took a change for the worse in farming. The opening up of the massive plains of arable lands in Canada and the USA, the arrival of frozen meat from New Zealand and Australia and canned food from South America, combined with a run of bad weather and poor harvests, led to an agricultural depression.

During this period many farmers and labourers moved away from the land so, unsurprisingly, farmhouses, buildings and cottages were left to rack and ruin. This depression is also reflected in Liddell's later journals. By 1880, his merchant's business was doing little in the way of trade, and page after page of the diary is covered with a gloomy single entry: 'Nil'. Gradually Liddell turned to fishing the rivers of Northumberland for consolation. For those who remained in the field there was diversification, and some ancestors may well have moved into market-gardening or the production of fresh meat and dairy products, which could be afforded by those making reasonable wages in the towns.

Farming limped through the twentieth century. Its products were in great demand during time of war when foreign markets were cut off. In some cases, sportsgrounds such as Sunderland's Ashbrooke ground turned over areas to market-gardening.

During the Second World War ladies of the land army were in great demand throughout the region, something that is reflected in oral histories being collected today.

One lecturer at an agricultural college just outside of Newcastle produced a pamphlet for national consumption during the war, entitled *Plots Against Hitler*. In this, he suggested that Northumberland often struggled with growing produce, with 'nine months of winter and three months of bad weather'. At the same time he noted that Northumbrians knew how best to use the conditions to advantage.

After the Second World War, the Ministry of Agriculture, Fisheries and Food played a more proactive role is assisting agriculture but many areas were badly affected by the great outbreak of foot and mouth in 2001. The effects of this continued to plague agriculture, in Cumbria in particular, well into the twenty-first century.

A number of other jobs related to agriculture but not, strictly speaking, part of the industry, remain of interest to the family historian. One is that of the miller. The remains of mills are scattered around the region and many of them have been turned into museums or heritage centres (see appendix 4, Museums). These mills were used for grinding corn to provide flour or animal feed but also for anything that needed solids to be ground to powder, such as flint for pottery and sand for glass.

On the north-east coast there were once over a hundred mills. A number of these have been preserved and three, in Tyne and Wear, today form part of an eight-mile walk taking in Whitburn, Cleadon and Fulwell mills. Whitburn Mill is a stone tower mill that was constructed in 1796 and is the oldest of the local tower mills. Cleadon Mill and Fulwell Mill both came into being during the early-nineteenth century.

Milling was a major industry in the nineteenth century and mills were a feature of the landscape from medieval times. Sacks of grain were bagged at the mill and sent out to local bakeries and different forms of grain were milled into usable products.

Fulwell Mill was commissioned in the early-nineteenth century and encases five floors. It worked as an actual windmill for over a century, before the sails were removed and a gas engine was put in. The mill continued to produce animal feed for local farmers for another half-century.

Agricultural Places

Early Cumbria showed signs of its future development as far back as pre-historic times with the early tending of cows, pigs and sheep. When agriculture is frequently presented as a downtrodden industry it is interesting to note past observers talking of relative prosperity in the area that forms modern Cumbria. As in Northumberland, demand frequently outstripped supply and this brought a great deal of work all year round for both men and women. A Board of Agriculture visitor in the late-eighteenth century noted this fact and the relatively high wages.

Commercial sheep-farming was established in the Kendal area by the Cistercian monks soon after the Norman Conquest and, for centuries, upland commons were strictly regulated and farmed. In the early days this was done under the manorial courts.

Fortunately there remain good sources for working and social life in Cumbria in the poetry and songs of the day, particularly in the former county of Cumberland, where Robert Anderson, the Cumberland Bard, spent a great deal of time in and around the villages near his native Carlisle. One of his songs, 'Young Susy', composed two hundred years ago, has a chorus that mentions virtually every task that was carried out by farm labourers of the time, including ploughing, sowing, threshing, dyking and mowing. Of equal interest is a poem called *The Upshot*, written by Cumbrian Mark Lonsdale, which describes in great detail life in the Solway village of Great Orton around 1780.

The history of Northumbrian agriculture is equally absorbing. Northumberland remains one of the most rural of counties, and agriculture was significant in shaping the lives of Northumbrian ancestors. Reports prepared for the government in the early-nineteenth century are helpful here. In the economic market, the labourer of Northumberland had the advantage over his southern counterpart: both male and female labour was in constant demand due to the lack of population.

Farmers had cottages that were rented out annually to the labourer, or hind. This labourer would bring with him a female who would be rewarded mainly in 'kind': agricultural produce, wool for spinning or yarn for blankets and stockings. The woman was a bondager who would work as and when required. Often this was the daughter or sister of the labourer, as the wife might be tied up in bringing up a family. In some cases, the hind could also board a woman if he did not have one. This system was not mentioned when agricultural reports were made in 1768, but those in the 1840s indicate that the system was settled by this time and possibly tied into new cultures such as the production of turnips.

There were also specialised agricultural industries such as those covered by Phil Huntley in a fascinating article in *The Northumbrian* (June/July 2005). He describes the remarkable strawberry industry on the town's High Moor (owned by the freemen of Alnwick). According to a newspaper report of the period, up to 6.3 tons of strawberries a day were transported from the railway station at Alnwick in the 1895 season. Women did most of the weeding and picking in this industry. The practice went on into the middle of the twentieth century and was passed on through many named families. It had died a natural death even before the station closed in the late-twentieth century.

There was also a linen trade but spinning was generally carried out for domestic purposes.

Further south, the famous agriculturalist Arthur Young noted the importance of agriculture in Historic County Durham when he paid a visit in the late-eighteenth century, and he had an interesting point to make:

> This then, is not a country of farmers, but a country of graziers, a country of pasture and not a country of the plough; and those who formerly managed the land here were not husbandmen, but herdsmen.

This was certainly the case in hillier areas. Elsewhere, the owners of big estates in Historic County Durham had been improving the rights of tenants from soon after the monasteries began to disappear, by arranging fairer leaseholds and copyholds.

Stuart times saw the rise of the gentry and move of Newcastle coal owners into the countryside. The enclosure of arable fields (if not the common pasture) was achieved in the seventeenth century, making agriculture a viable business.

By the eighteenth century there had been an impressive expansion in agriculture and an increase in the numbers employed producing food, for their own needs as well as those of the pitmen.

Historic County Durham, of course, included parts that are now in the modern Tees Valley, where the remnants of an agricultural past are still on view. Medieval farm practice can still be seen today in places such as the small township of Brierton between Hartlepool and the A19 road from Tyneside to the Tees. Now one large farm, Brierton developed from a settlement through a series of smaller farms to what it is today. It is surrounded by three large fields, which are little different from the three fields of the ancient system practised before the agricultural revolution.

Close by is the village of Elwick, a typical English green village reflecting the old farming and subsistence economy. This is based on a medieval agricultural settlement planned by the Normans. It has retained its fine village green, and nearby there are signs of a hall, fishponds and the old ridge-and-furrow method of farming.

The area, connected to both the de Brus (of Robert the Bruce) family and the Neville family, has changed relatively little over the centuries. Many villages, like those on the Solway in Cumbria, were built around farms, the buildings of which remain central to the community today.

Darlington and the surrounding area also played a significant role in agricultural developments. By the Middle Ages, Darlington had become a flourishing industrial town, important for the export of wool and the weaving and dyeing of cloth. In the eighteenth century, Darlington's thriving market was at the centre of a local agricultural revolution. The Collings family, based around Darlington, built on the work of the famous breeder Robert Bakewell by developing shorthorn cattle – according to one observer – 'the reason why the Northern Dales were the home of this important cattle breed for 300 years'.

Finding More

Agriculture was different from other industries in that work was often seasonal and the workers scattered around. This has often been given as a reason why it took such a long time for agricultural workers to unite in a union. This solitary way of life also means that little has survived in the way of individual employment records except, perhaps, in the case of the very big estates and even then the mention of specific names is likely to be a case of pot luck.

For those researching individual farm workers, experience teaches that parish registers, censuses and civil certificates tend to provide references to abodes which can, in turn, be linked to farm employment with the help of local small-scale maps. These can usually be found in most of the major North Country archives and local study centres.

Farmers and landowners can also be traced through similar material as well as the local parish rate lists, tithe lists and maps, electoral rolls and poll books (see chapters 7, Government and 9, Religion). In the case of landowners and farmers, it is always worth looking at general archive indexes and, at a national level, at manorial document registers in the National Register of Archives at The National Archives.

The Berwick office of the Northumberland Record Office also has papers relating to the Ford estate, and the manor of Broughton in Furness is well served by the Barrow office of the Cumbria Record Office.

Individual family farming records can sometimes be found, such as those of the Ewart Family of The Knowe, Bewcastle, and the Hudleston family of Hutton John, which are both kept at Carlisle.

Records of the Pennyman family of Ormesby Hall, Yorkshire, turn up in the Teesside Archives.

The Northumberland Archive at Woodhorn has extensive records for the Culley family, who were farmers and improvers in the eighteenth and nineteenth centuries. An early George Culley was a contemporary of the famous agriculturalist Arthur Young, and a later George Culley was a provider of agricultural information to the government. It is an interesting observation on rural life, perhaps, that the later George Culley appears in the 1881 census of Fowberry, Northumberland, with six servants and living next door to John Lowlie, 'ag lab' age fifty-eight, and his wife, Jane. Next to them is James Robson, aged sixty-eight, general labourer, with his son, an 'ag lab', and his daughter, a farm servant. Two doors down from them is 23-year-old William Black, a shepherd.

Flesh on the Bones

The agricultural way of life is featured in a number of museums and heritage centres. In Cumbria, The Museum of Lakeland Life at Abbot Hall in Kendal has exhibits relating to agriculture in both Lakeland and the Rough Fell Country.

The Helena Thompson Museum at Workington also has a newly installed display concerning the World Ploughing Organisation. It presents in detail the aims and objectives of the organisation, and the history of ploughing and plough-making in general, as well as relating the story of how the world-wide organisation grew out of the agricultural shows and ploughing matches held at Workington after the Second World War.

Also in Cumbria there are a number of museums dedicated to mills, such as Eskdale Mill in West Cumbria. This is a cornmill dating back to the sixteenth century.

In Penrith there is a small museum which has a feature on watermills. Further south in the former Yorkshire area, Farfield Mill at Sedbergh has evidence for tracing the history of the wool industry in the area.

Also in the Lake District is Dove Cottage, famed for its connection with the Wordsworth family. This is essentially a rural Lakeland cottage of the late-eighteenth century although, because of the importance of its chief residents, it cannot be considered absolutely typical.

The home of the famous engraver Thomas Bewick at Cherryburn near Stocksfield in Northumberland is also of interest to those researching agricultural heritage. Although Bewick gained fame for his art, he was in many ways a typical rural Northumbrian of the eighteenth century. His family had money yet he enjoyed spending time with his family's workers and was very keen on all Northumbrian traditions, especially song and music. The birthplace house celebrates Bewick's life and works, and his readable autobiography is worth the effort for anyone with an interest in rural Northumberland during this period.

The North of England Museum at Beamish in Modern County Durham is best known for its industrial exhibits but in its Home Farm and Pockerley Manor also features agricultural heritage.

Many of the small museums scattered around the region and listed in the index also feature extensive exhibits related to agriculture.

Finally, this seems a suitable place to draw attention to the agriculturally dependent market-towns. In a basically rural economy, the market-town has an important role to play, and they (or their remnants, now submerged by industrial growth) are to be found in virtually every part of the region.

Stockton, close to the Tees, is a fine example of a former market-town. Incorporated as such by Bishop Bek in 1310, it has retained its market-town character despite centuries of change. Hexham, in Northumberland, centrally placed in the Tyne Valley, still possesses all the elements of a market-town.

Other fine examples are Brampton, in Cumbria, and Alston, on the top of the Pennines. Keswick, although much altered by tourism, has the feel of a market-town – the list is almost endless – and the old Westmorland towns of Kirkby Stephen, Kirkby Lonsdale and Appleby are difficult to exclude, as are Durham, Darlington, Barnard Castle, Hartlepool, Stockton, Sedgefield, Staindrop and Wolsingham. Many of these market-towns were to play important roles in of the poor laws after 1834 (see chapter 9, Local Government).

Chapter Four

IRON AND STEEL MANUFACTURE AND ENGINEERING

U p until the industrial revolution of the eighteenth and nineteenth centuries, those involved in the iron industry were likely to be found in rural surroundings near to the source of iron, running water and the wood for charcoal, which was used to smelt the iron. In this respect, the early metal manufacturing industry in the North Country followed the national pattern.

Among the earliest of iron manufacturers in the North were the monks of Furness Abbey in Cumbria. They smelted iron with wood in the thirteenth century. Despite such activity, an iron manufactory in the area was not necessarily good news for local miners. Until as late as the nineteenth century British iron was often considered of poor quality, and imported iron was used. Newcastle was among the ports that benefited from imports of the metal.

By the time the agricultural and industrial revolutions were gathering pace, the majority of ironworkers were to be found in large towns or cities. Processed iron was now in demand for farm machinery, railway building and development, coal and textile machinery and machinery for metal manufacture itself. As a result, metal manufactories of various sizes could be found in towns throughout the region and coking coal began to replace wood-based charcoal as the main fuel.

These 'factories' tended to be set up close to the new fuel source, so areas around the Tyne and Tees and in the west of Historic County Durham joined Lancashire beyond the Sands and the Cumbrian coast as major areas for iron manufacture. As large-scale steel production followed, later in the nineteenth century, it was natural that the same areas should reap further rewards.

Manufacturing Metal

The role played by the manufacture of iron and steel goods in North Country life may be best understood by reference to the ironmasters who made things happen across the region. In this instance, time rather than regional geography will serve most usefully as a guide.

North-Eastern ironmaster Ambrose Crowley was one of the first to begin manufacture on a large scale on the eastern side. He came up from southern England and settled in Sunderland in 1682. In 1690 he moved to Swalwell and Winlaton on the Tyne and used coal and wood for smelting.

The renowned Wilkinson family, most notably 'Iron-Mad' John and Isaac, mentioned as pioneering ironmasters in every relevant school textbook, had firm roots in the region. An iron business connected with this family developed at Backbarrow in southern Lakeland in the early-eighteenth century. Here they produced grates and cooking pots, and John himself lies buried in an iron coffin at Lindale.

Also in the southern Lakes, Isaac Hazlehurst of Poakabeck set up as a steel refiner in the nineteenth century. He was born at Wellington in Shropshire in 1806 and his wife came from Madeley near Coalbrookdale – the cradle of the revolution in metal manufacture.

In 1839, H W Schneider came to nearby Barrow-in-Furness as a young dealer in iron. In 1850 he discovered large deposits of iron, and erected blast furnaces at Barrow, which by 1876 overlooked one of the largest steelworks in the world.

The discovery of workable iron in the Cleveland Hills had much to do with developments around the Tees. In 1850 German Henry Bolckow and Englishman John Vaughan opened their mills and furnaces on the riverbanks and, in the 1870s, brought in Bessemer converters.

There were also numerous smaller-scale projects. Charles Reed, for example, started a small iron manufactory in Sunderland in the 1860s. He came from the same area of Portsmouth as Henry Cort, the famous metal manufacturer. Reed's son later expanded the business and ended up employing a hundred men.

Because many North Country ancestors were involved in the process of metal manufacture, it is necessary to understand a little about the actual process of production. After the iron ore had been mined and sorted out from the rock, it was smelted in a blast furnace and the resultant molten metal poured into special moulds called pigs; the result was known as 'pig iron'. From here the pig iron could be made into cast iron, which was brittle and hard. The other form of iron was wrought iron, which was firmer and easier to mould.

The making of steel starts with the iron process, then necessitates the addition of carbon to provide a metal as hard as cast iron, as supple as wrought iron and strong.

In the steel industry the inventions of both Huntsman's crucible and

Bessemer's converter proved key developments. In addition the researches of London magistrates' clerk, Sidney Gilchrist-Thomas was of particular significance to the North Country. He found a way of lining a steel converter so British-mined iron ore could be used, and was partly responsible for the resulting growth of the Tees Valley and Furness manufactories.

As with the other great regional industries, official records often describe those who worked in an iron or steelworks simply as a 'labourers'. This can be particularly unhelpful in areas near the coast, where 'labourers' may equally have been involved in dock work. Fortunately some census enumerators and official scribes did take time to fully log the occupation as 'labourer in the steelworks/ironworks'.

A principal cause of generalisation in logging was the simple fact that metal manufacture did involve a great deal of general labour, particularly in cleaning up after production and getting rid of waste, or 'slag', which was part of the process.

There were occasions when individual jobs were singled out. Anybody in a role of responsibility might be referred to as a 'foreman', and the role of the 'puddler' seemed to be one that frequently warranted special mention. Puddling was an important part of the process of iron production from the late-eighteenth century. It entailed constantly stirring the molten iron with a long-handled spoon placed through a window into the furnace. This process improved the quality of iron but it would have been hot, dirty work stirring the iron, then heaving out the puddle-balls for flattening. The term 'iron puddler' turns up in 1881 census for Tyneside and on official individual documentation in the Hartlepool area.

The term 'iron moulder' was another in use and is mentioned in the 1861 census for Gateshead. In addition, some reference might be made to those involved in forge work, or in operating a specific machine such as a steam hammer, or in transport, either removing the finished metal or taking the waste to the slag heap. The slag heap was a prominent feature of steel-working towns and cities because the hot waste lit up the skyline at night. In West Hartlepool the steelmaking area was nicknamed 'Wagga' and the slag heap's glow known as the 'Wagga Moon'.

The invaluable research of historian Ivy Pinchbeck in the 1920s allows us to learn something about life for the women workers in metal manufacture. In the early days, wives would help their husbands around the forge. Working the bellows was one of their tasks here. Even when the work became heavier and more industrialised, women continued to be employed. Pinchbeck records that fifty women were employed at the Beamish forges in County Durham in the second quarter of the nineteenth century, and children as young as seven were still used to operate the bellows.

The experience of metalworkers in the Poakabeck and Martin area of South Cumbria makes for a particularly good case study. In 1851, eight of the residents of Martin were described as iron puddlers and research indicates that a small ironworks was set up here sometime between 1840 and 1850. There were others in the village who were also connected to the industry: a master iron roller and three tradesmen, as well as four forgemen.

The works here were destined for a very short life and became overshadowed by the significant developments at Barrow. Among these came the damming up of the local stream to provide a decent water supply for the growing town. This must have brought production at Poakabeck to an end and little evidence now remains of this briefly flourishing industry.

Metal Manufacturing Districts

Local historians throughout the region make claims for the international importance of their own local metal manufacturing industry and, taken in its entirety, the North Country certainly led the world in metal manufacture.

In Northumberland and Historic County Durham alone (which includes the complexes around the Tees), thirty-nine per cent of national iron production took place in 1913. In the same year steel ingots and castings produced in the North-East generally made up twenty-seven per cent of the total for Great Britain.

Iron and steel manufacture formed a large part of the Cumbrian economy. Beside that of the Wilkinson family at Backbarrow, there was a furnace at nearby Duddon Bridge. There were also foundries at Maryport and Lowca near Whitehaven. Cannons were produced at the latter in the eighteenth century before production moved to steam engines and iron gear. Two railway engines, Dolgoch and Talyllyn, were built here in the mid-nineteenth century for the Talyllyn railway and these were later to be immortalised in a children's book written by The Reverend W Awdry, who wrote *Thomas the Tank Engine*.

The railway was also the making of nearby Workington, where metal manufacturers gained a reputation for the production of rails. The Workington Haematite Company was also set up in 1856 to make pig iron from local ore. Steelmaking, using the Bessemer method, began in the 1870s and lasted for a century. The manufacture of rails at Workington continued into the present century, outlasting steelmaking by some thirty years.

After an eighteenth-century fling in the iron production market, Maryport established the Maryport Hematite Company in 1870. Business was initially good and there were six furnaces in operation within two years. Recession took its toll in 1882; bankruptcy loomed and the company was taken over by the Maryport Hematite Iron and Steel Company Ltd, which survived until 1891 before going into receivership. The iron works were closed permanently in the 1920s.

Developments at Barrow-in-Furness have been dealt with above. At nearby Millom, there were the ironworks of the Cumberland Iron Mining and Smelting Company to complement the iron-ore mine at Hodbarrow. Blast

Barrow steelworks just before demolition.

furnaces were established here in 1867 and Millom soon had a reputation for the production of top-quality pig iron.

In Northumberland, Swinney Brothers of Morpeth employed over a hundred men around 1900 and built everything from bridges to lampposts, galley stoves, flood gullies and blank shells in wartime.

The Crowley works on Tyneside eventually produced iron and steel goods and employed several hundred workmen. Palmer's works supplied the ship-building trade.

Consett, in the west of Modern County Durham, was a vital iron-manufacturing town. Set up in 1841 to satisfy the demands of the railways, it continued production well into the twentieth century. The local coal was ideal for smelting and Consett immediately became one of the biggest producers in the country, with fourteen blast furnaces plus mills for puddling, hammering and rolling. The population of 10,000 had come from all corners of Great Britain after the census 1841.

Middlesbrough, today in the Tees Valley, was a major player in the field of metal manufacture but Bolckow and Vaughan were not the only ones operating around the river. The Stockton Iron Works, Portrack Iron Works, Teesdale Iron Works, Pease and Partners, Tees Iron Works and Normanby Iron Works were all working on iron production at around the same time or earlier.

In the later nineteenth-century, competition from abroad forced a number of Teesside's ironworks to amalgamate. This resulted in the emergence of Dorman Long, who in the 1880s switched to steel production and by the turn of the century had added a bridge and construction works and steel erection businesses to its growing empire. By 1904, Dorman Long's three plants had a capacity of about 450,000 tons.

In nearby West Hartlepool, metal manufacture developed to become an integral part of the economy, with much of the iron and steel produced supplying the shipbuilding industry. In the mid-century, the firm of Pile and Spence was in control; by the turn of the century, the whole complex lay in the hands of Sir Christopher Furness. The West Hartlepool industry then became part of the larger Durham Iron and Steel Company.

The story of North Country metal manufacture is one of highs and lows: long-term problems appeared on the horizon as early as 1880 when other countries, notably Germany and the USA, began to challenge Britain's control of the world market.

Although changes were made in the industry, the British tended to stick to old and outdated methods of production. Its decline in influence was arrested somewhat by an increase in demand during the two world wars of the twentieth century but the decrease in production which followed both was to be expected. By the late-twentieth century, the writing was on the wall for most of British metal manufacture and many northern communities have suffered in consequence.

Even in the inter-war years, where there was still a demand for steel it was mostly for lighter or strip steel for the new industries and this had become the province of central and eastern England.

Engineering is perhaps the most difficult industry to explore. It often has intricate and close links to iron and steel as well as shipbuilding and other industries, so references to specific forms of engineering appear elsewhere in the book.

Early forms of heavy engineering in the region encompassed work on both the stationary steam engine and the steam locomotive; there were other forms of constructional engineering too, most notably the building of viaducts and bridges. One of the most successful of the early engineering firms was Hawks, Crawshay and Company. Established in 1747 as the Gateshead Iron Company, it was responsible for the building of the renowned High Level Bridge across the Tyne in 1849 and could also have been included in the section on iron and steel manufacture.

The mining industry too required engineering support: the Dunston Engine Works Company at Gateshead was engaged for years in the production of winding and coal-cleansing machinery and cages.

Around the Tees, engineering really began to take off in the middle of the nineteenth century. The Teesdale Iron Works came into operation in 1840; with take-overs and additions, it had become Head Wrightson by 1866.

Later, there were developments in lighter industry and, by the turn of the nineteenth century, the Reyrolle Electrical Machinery Works was in operation at Hebburn on the Tyne.

During the inter-war years, electrical engineering was the main growth area in the manufacturing section of the regional economy. Later, support industries grew up in new towns such as Newton Aycliffe, Peterlee and New Washington (later Washington New Town and now simply Washington).

Older towns also developed trading estates in which a variety of electrical goods were produced in the post-war years.

Finding More

Although not as extensive as the records relating to shipbuilding and mining, material concerning iron and steel manufacture still survives in a number of regional repositories.

The Whitehaven office of the Cumbrian Archives Service has records from Heathcotes (Cleator Moor) Ltd, iron founders and Whitehaven Hematite Iron Company. Some of these date back to the mid-nineteenth century.

The records of the Curwen family of Workington Hall and Cumberland United Steel also contain material of interest in this field.

The Barrow office maintains the records of Hart Jackson and Son, solicitors, of Ulverston. These contain a number of documents relating to individual metal manufacturers. So too do the Furness Estates records of the Duke of Buccleuch.

Material relating to the Millom and Askham Hematite Iron Co Ltd and the Charcoal Iron Company of Backbarrow can also be found at Barrow.

The Northumberland Archives keeps a range of documents concerning the Bedlington Ironworks (which had early links to the Stockton and Darlington Railway) as well as some connected to Iron and Steel Workers' Associations.

The Berwick office has material relating to the Forge and Iron factory at Ford in North Northumberland.

Some of the most interesting records concerning iron and steel manufacture in the region turn up in the Tyne and Wear Archives. They are among the papers of the solicitors Thomas Bell and Sons.

In these records, the ironworks of the Felling Chemical Company appear on a number of occasions, as do those of H L Pattinson and Partners, the famous Hawks and Company 'in the parish of Gateshead', the Gateshead Park Ironworks and the Bishopwearmouth Iron Company on Wearside.

Tees Valley records are also extensive, as might be expected. The Teesside Archives records cover, among others, Head Wrightson and Company, the British Steel Corporation, W Richards and Sons Ltd, Ironfounders, and Middlesbrough's Ayresome Ironworks. The ironworks at Cargo Fleet and Ormesby also feature heavily.

Flesh on the Bones

Generally speaking, there are few places which dedicate a great amount of space to the history of metal manufacture although museums in the major towns and cities in the region, which supported iron and steel, usually have some displays on the development of the industry.

The Helena Thompson Museum at Workington displays goods connected with the iron and steel industry alongside examples of the minerals used in the production, and Barrow Dock Museum has objects and information relating to the Barrow Steelworks.

Perhaps the most interesting metal manufacturing centre in the region lies at Derwentcote in Modern County Durham – between Hamsterley and Rowlands Gill and close to the steel town of Consett. Although only open for limited periods during the summer months, the steel furnace there is well worth a visit. At Derwentcote, steel was manufactured by the cementation process. According to the guide this is 'unique – the country's earliest most complex steelmaking furnace to have survived intact.' The process shown here dominated British steelmaking until the early-nineteenth century.

The Museum of Hartlepool and the Dorman Museum, Middlesbrough, both have material relating to the production of iron and steel.

Chapter Five

TRANSPORT

In most regional books, a chapter on transport may be classified as purely social history: not so here! The north-eastern area of the North Country, in particular, is heralded as the cradle of the railway. At the same time, the development of export markets for coal, iron and steel and the craving for imports coincided with the growth of shipbuilding to turn shipping itself into a key industry on both coasts.

The North Country also possessed large rivers, which provided work for those who lived near them (although geography dictated that the region would take little part in the canal boom).

In short, railway, river and sea transport afforded a way of life to many of our North Country ancestors.

The Railway

The birth of the railway in the North Country is directly linked to the need for a better method of transporting coal. Initially the intent was simply to use the railway as a method of delivering coal from the pithead to the nearest stretch of water; later developments ensured that the railway became a complete service in itself, transporting the material almost 'from door to door'.

The early industrial revolution saw the growth of a system of wooden wagon ways throughout the region – simple roads at first but later employing wooden rails and complex systems of levers for changing lines. A well-preserved section of such a line was discovered recently when redevelopment was taking place at the former Lambton Coke Works near Sunderland.

Under this system, the coal was carried in a truck with a horse and brake; the road was inclined so the wagon could travel downwards with little guidance and return up with the aid of a horse. All this was quite labour-intensive and many men and boys in Far Northern coalmining communities would have worked as drivers or brakesmen. These could be dangerous occupations, as Geordie Ridley, writer of 'The Blaydon Races' found out to his cost. His leg was badly injured when a wagon fell on him, forcing him into full-time work as an as an entertainer and writer of local songs.

As steam technology developed, the choice of method for coal transport lay between a static engine hauling wagons by rope or by a movable locomotive or 'self-propelling engine'. Although the locomotive eventually won the race, the other method was used extensively and there is still evidence for this activity in a number of places in the North-East – especially around the margins of the Wear at Bowes and Warden Law.

Whether through pure endeavour or good fortune, George Stephenson, a Tyneside man, took most credit for the victory of the locomotive. Despite his Tyneside roots, he is most readily associated with the stretch of line from Stockton to Darlington constructed for the purpose of carrying coal and general goods.

Early sketches and paintings show that in the case of the Stockton and Darlington, people were an afterthought – transported in what were essentially enclosed highway carriages on rails. The Stockton and Darlington Railway was just the beginning, and the commercial prospect offered by goods and passengers led to an erratic explosion of railway-building or 'railway mania'.

The result was a great deal of work in construction, and the loose term 'railway worker' came to be used for those building and working on the railway system. These workers, or navvies, formed a hard-living group and there were often disturbances. On one occasion during the building of the Hartlepool dock and railway complex, the Riot Act was read and combatants were threatened with the militia.

In Cumbria, the creation of the Lancaster and Penrith Railway brought chaos to the Cumbrian market-town. At the annual meeting of the poor-law officials in Penrith in 1845, local bard John Rayson sang his own song about the consequent demise of the local ladies. The culprits he named in the 'railway race' were masons, quarrymen and navvies and they hailed from Connaught and Derry and also included 'Highlandmen, Manxmen, Lankies and Scotchmen from north of the Tweed'. In a note accompanying the published song, Rayson adds that the navvies 'were in the habit of leaving women (not wives) and children to be maintained at the parish expense'.

The peak of railway building came in the 1840s, by which time railway companies of different sizes had been set up all over the region. Many of the systems they built put industry's needs before those of the passengers. The line from Sunderland to Hartlepool, for example, was criss-crossed with colliery lines; one passenger, in 1851, said a journey on it reminded him of Benjamin Bolus's medicine' – to be well shaken while taken'.

These railways continued to expand throughout the nineteenth century and still served many rural areas well into the twentieth century. Since the 1960s and, in some cases earlier, many significant routes have disappeared, the links between Sunderland and Durham and along the Solway from Carlisle among them.

Railway Places

There are many places in the North Country with important railway connections. In Cumbria, work began on the building of a railway in the Maryport area in 1837, the first section of line carrying coal from the West Cumberland pits becoming operational in 1841. With the arrival of the Maryport and Carlisle Railway, a locomotive and carriage construction works at Grasslot to the south of the town was established.

Around Barrow, the Furness railway became key to the import and export of material, and the Lowca works near Whitehaven produced many light locomotives used in industry.

Carlisle was one of the most important junctions in the country and boasted a number of engine sheds popular with trainspotters well into the twentieth century. Workington had a long-term reputation for producing iron and steel rails (see chapter 4, Iron and Steel Manufacture for more on Cumbrian links). The railway also opened up the Lake District to visitors.

A vital link across the entire region was established when the argument between canal and rail was won with the development of the economically key Newcastle to Carlisle Railway, passing from east to west.

In Northumberland and on Tyneside, the Stephensons and others beavered away at laying down early roots. Stephenson's works in Newcastle itself was highly active in the nineteenth century and has links back to the famous *Rocket*. William Hedley worked on the *Puffing Billy*.

On Wearside the development of the railway surrounded stations north and south of the river. In the very early days there was no railway bridge across the Wear and passengers had to alight at Monkwearmouth then cross into the town by foot in order to take a train southwards down the coast.

Modern County Durham was criss-crossed by a number of significant railways and contains the pioneering railway town of Shildon.

When the idea of the Stockton and Darlington Railway was being promoted in the early-1820s, Stockton already had a reputation for the export of stockings, linen, wheat and lead. The railway was finally opened in September 1825. Stephenson drove *Locomotion No 1* with fellow engineer, Timothy Hackworth (from Shildon) as guard.

Middlesbrough also lays claim to being the first town created by the railway: the 1830 railway extension to its Coal Dock made its development possible. Further north, the old fishing port of Hartlepool was saved from extinction by the railway and neighbouring West Hartlepool created by it.

The Hartlepools' developments came after abortive efforts to build a successful port at the mouth of the Tees. Attentions turned to the old town, then a battle with the Stockton and Darlington Railway Company led to the birth of a Hartlepool (West) Company and ultimately to the construction of the town of West Hartlepool itself.

As the century wore on, another battle developed for control of the key East

Coast line with 'Railway King' George Hudson and West Hartlepool's Ralph Ward Jackson involved. Hudson eventually won the day.

Shipping

If the sea inlets are included, the region's coasts stretch in the west from Carlisle down to Morecambe and in the east from Berwick to the Tees. It was thus natural that ports should develop and that the activities of making the docks, manning them and sailing the ships to and from them should be taken up by many of the inhabitants.

In medieval times, the eastern ports of Berwick, Newcastle and Hartlepool were regarded as ideal points for military provisioning (see chapter 10, Military and Warfare). Whitehaven and Maryport on the west coast linked into growing westward trade routes in the eighteenth century.

On the east coast too, the Tyne was a significant river from Roman times onwards whereas Sunderland, Hartlepool and West Hartlepool developed as the industrial revolution of the eighteenth and nineteenth centuries gave a boost to the existing ports and brought about the creation of new ones.

The number of jobs created by all these changes was considerable; ancestors can be found on certificates and in censuses as labourers constructing the docks or as dock workers loading and unloading the vessels throughout the nineteenth century. Some of these labouring jobs were quite specific. The coal trimmer, for example, was involved in trimming or evening out the coal being loaded on collier ships to ensure that the vessel stayed in balance, and this occupation was frequently noted in official documents.

Then there were those North Country men who actually went to sea and appear in documentation as seamen or mariners, ship's mates or master mariners – a term used for those who were certificated as mates or captains of trading vessels. As the vessels turned from sail to steam, ancestors could also be ship's engineers.

Although the role of master mariner carried some kudos, the captains of smaller vessels could lead fairly humdrum lives. In 1885, the *Spero*, belonging to the Pelton Steamship Company, spent her time chugging from the Tyne to Greenwich, Dublin and Amsterdam. With such short passages, her captain spent almost as much time at home as he did away.

Crews could often be drawn from all over the country although South Shields became famed for its resident foreign seamen (see chapter 14, Movement).

There was a decline in the general number of British merchant seamen in the late-twentieth century as shipping became less labour-intensive and more and more foreign crews came to be employed.

Shipping Places

In the nineteenth century both Maryport and Whitehaven in Cumbria seemed destined for great things as they built up shipping links with Ireland and the New World. Success continued to some extent in the nineteenth century. The Holme Shipping Line owned and operated sixteen sailing vessels from Maryport in the 1870s – a number of them built on the Wear. The town was also the birthplace of Thomas Henry Ismay of *Titanic* and White Star Line fame.

Maryport's experience gives some indication of the way trade worked. General cargoes went to Australia and returned with wool. Rails were taken across to Canada and the vessels returned with grain and timber. Unfortunately the sandbanks and shallow waters of the Solway ensured that progress did not continue into the days of the larger steamships.

Blyth, in Northumberland, blossomed as a port in the late-nineteenth century although in the 1850s and 1860s it was not much larger than many local villages. In 1851, there were some 118 sailing vessels owned in the port. By 1874, the number had topped 200.

Walter Runciman's book *Collier Brigs and Their Sailors* deals almost exclusively with ships from the port of Blyth. One chapter lists local casualties between 1865 and 1891 such as the *Elpis* of Blyth, which was lost off Porthcawl with nine hands on 25 November 1865. Runciman's book also contains an interesting list of all the Blyth-owned vessels for the period, and their owners, shipmasters and place of building.

Most of the vessels sailing out of Blyth at the time were small brigs weighing 200 or 300 tons and the majority of them older vessels built in Sunderland some years earlier.

Blyth has yet another claim to fame. It was an important centre for the collection of sea shanties, and many of the versions learned in twentieth-century schools including 'What Shall We Do With The Drunken Sailor?' and 'Billy Boy' were collected here, and often adapted by the collectors for the sake of propriety!

On Tyneside, the pitmen dug the coal, the keelmen transported it to the ships and Tyneside mariners took it up and down the coast and overseas.

The Quayside at Newcastle, today an international centre for nightlife, was once a hive of industrial activity with a mass of warehouses, and the Tyne's end-of-the-line importance is recognised in the old mariner's rhyme:

> *First the Dudgeon then the Spurn*
> *Flamborough Head next in turn*
> *Twenty miles north to the Whitby Light*
> *The Old Man says, 'We'll be in Shields tonight'*

In South Shields itself, the customs house, a successful theatre today, was central to trade and has amongst its buildings the nearby Board of Trade offices, where the master mariners used to sign in. The building also hosts a mortuary, where bodies washed up in the Tyne or removed from vessels were placed – a solemn reminder of the toughness of life on the waters.

On the Wear, port improvements were made in the eighteenth century to accommodate larger ships coming into Sunderland. This was essential, as, in contrast to the Tyne, the sea-bound reaches of the Wear are narrow and squeezed by cliffs. The changes were not made for coal export alone. By this time salt, glass and pottery had also entered the equation.

Slightly down the coast, Lord Londonderry built Seaham Harbour for the export of coal from his collieries and, for many years, West Hartlepool thrived on the export of coal and the import of timber for the construction of pit props.

Inland Water Transport

While North Country railways and shipping are deserving of special attention, canals are not. There were some canals in the region – mainly in the south-west in the areas around Kendal and Ulverston; there was talk too of a huge canal from coast to coast which, for a short period, laid down roots between Carlisle and Port Carlisle. Despite these small ventures, the coming of the railway and the economic failure of the Leeds to Liverpool Canal, which passed over terrain similar to that in the North Country, soon killed off any prospects of canal construction.

The North Country lay beyond the pale of the St Andrew's Cross that linked Hull and Bristol, London and Liverpool and revolved around the axis of Birmingham. In consequence, there may have been some canal workers in the region but they were few and far between.

The same could not be said of the river workers. Certainly in the years prior to railway mania, the Tyne, Wear and Tees were of considerable economic importance although the Tees was always a river with problems. It remained a notoriously difficult river to navigate and, with the onset of the industrial revolution, early ports upstream at Yarm and Stockton began to struggle as ships grew in size and the river silted up.

The rivers were of particular importance to the early coal trade. After the coal had been transported along the wagon ways, most of it ended up at a riverside, especially along the Tyne and Wear. From here, it was taken downstream in keelboats to a place where the coal could be loaded for sea transport. Such transportation was highly labour-intensive and many men were occupied in it until railways began to replace both the horse-drawn wagon and the keelboat.

There was an art to working in the keelboats, which usually had a crew of four. Contemporary songs and ballads, although often poking fun at the keelmen, do actually give a vivid picture of a keelman's working life from the loading of coal on the keel to unloading of it onto a sea-bound vessel.

The Tyne was alive with keelboats. A report of 1725 described the wooden staithes on the riverbank and the boats themselves – 'lighters or keels' – that took the coal to the sea-bound ships 'chiefly about Shields'. According to the writer of the report, there were some 800 keels on the Tyne at the time and every keel employed four men. Payment depended not merely on the amount of coal transported from the keel but also on the height that the receiving vessel was standing in the water.

Jack Crawford from Sunderland, the hero of Camperdown, started on the keelboats as a boy in the 1780s and returned to the job after years in the merchant navy and Royal Navy. According to biographers, his job in later life consisted of filling the baskets with coal for transfer from the keel to the sea-going vessel. His son, though born in London while Crawford was in the navy, later worked on the Tyne and is recorded in the census as a 'waterman'.

The rivers were also used for the transport of general goods and hosted a number of ferries in the days before massive bridge building. During such times, the job of ferryman was not uncommon. Other important river jobs included pilot and foyboatman, and these jobs were often passed down through well-known and well-respected families.

Up to the end of the eighteenth century, the first bridge inland from the coast crossed the Wear some ten miles inland close to Chester-le-Street.

The Wear crossing at Chester-le-Street.

Roads and Bridges

The North Country was never an easy region either to access or to cross, as travellers and traders over the centuries have discovered. Its roads, running from Flinters Gill near Dent in the south-west of the region to Salters Road in Gosforth, Newcastle, and beyond, served a variety of purposes. They were often poor, and neglected to such an extent that the sea was considered a safer and more efficient route. As in other parts of the country, the former Roman roads were the best ones, in some cases right up to the nineteenth century.

With the Pennines bisecting the region and the gaps in the chain uniting it, the major road systems have basically stayed the same over the centuries. The A1/A1M route marks the east-coast link between the South and Edinburgh, the A6/M6 that between the South and Glasgow. The A66 from Scotch Corner to Penrith and the A69 from Newcastle to Carlisle remain the favoured cross-country routes.

Before the advent of the bypass and the motorway, even before the car and the railway, these routes created favourite watering-holes – Kendal, Penrith and Carlisle in the west – Darlington, Durham, Chester-le-Street, Morpeth, Alnwick and a host of others in the east.

Such was the nature of this dual route up and down the coasts that those involved in the Jacobite Rebellions of the eighteenth century had to make the decision as to which route to take from Scotland. In both cases (1715 and 1745), they came down by the west, heading for a Catholic Lancashire where they believed their cause would be taken up.

Tyneside folk were seen as supporters of the Protestant 'German' kings; in many quarters it is believed that the use of the phrase 'they're all German Geordie's men' by the Earl of Marr led eventually to the common adoption of

A view from the A66 into Yorkshire.

the term 'Geordie' for people living in and around Newcastle.These rebellions led to a further development – the building of the military road from Newcastle to Carlisle along the line of Hadrian's Wall.

General Wade, conscious of being unable to move troops swiftly from one side of the country to the other to stop invaders, was behind its construction, and modern school textbooks are now acknowledging Wade's work alongside that of more famous road builders Telford, Macadam and Metcalfe.

The main roads were carried by a series of key bridges from Croft near Darlington in the east to Eamont near Penrith in the west. Further north the bridges at Stanwix in Carlisle and across the Tyne at Newcastle were also significant.

Roads and bridges brought work for our North Country ancestors in their building and repairing. Prior to the railway, and in some cases for years after, they led travellers and their horses and carriages to hotels and inns, which were themselves providers of local employment.

The toll roads also bought work. The uncle of Tyneside diarist Joseph Liddell looked after a tollgate on the outskirts of Sunderland, and Joseph himself noted the annual hiring out of tolls on roads and bridges in his diary.

Tyneside in general, and Newcastle in particular, remains renowned for its many bridges (a claim which could be equally matched by Gateshead on the other side!). Numerous bridges have crossed the Tyne since a settlement first appeared there from the first Roman bridge to the modern Millennium 'blinking eye' bridge, now a major tourist attraction.

Perhaps the two most significant bridges across the Tyne are the High Level Bridge constructed under the guidance of Robert Stephenson, son of George, in the mid-nineteenth century, and the more famous Tyne Bridge, or King George Bridge, which dates from the early-twentieth century. It was opened by George V in 1924 and is said to be the prototype for the Sydney Harbour Bridge.

Finding More

There appear to be few railway records of direct interest to family historians in the region. Most of them seem to be related to the legislation surrounding the actual purchase of land and building of the railways.

The Cumbria Archives at Carlisle contains the Senhouse family papers dealing with the Maryport and Carlisle Railway as well as some British Rail records. The Kendal branch has much material relating to the Cumbria Railway Association. Barrow has some British Rail material and some relevant solicitors' papers (as does the Whitehaven office).

The papers in the Northumberland Archives seem to deal mainly with the construction and engineering of colliery railways, and the Tyne and Wear Archives has railway maps and plans plus some LNER and British Rail material.

Teesside Archives keeps the records of the Cleveland Railway and has some interesting material on the links between Ormesby Hall and early railways.

Maritime records tend to be fuller. In general, information on ordinary sailors and officers in the merchant marine are best consulted at national level. The records for such people are excellent from the middle of the nineteenth century onwards and The National Archives at Kew and the National Maritime Museum at Greenwich both have records of considerable help to researchers in this field.

Usually, knowledge of a name, birth date (approximate) and birthplace can gain access to the person's seaman's number and record at sea. Depending on the time when they served at sea, this can lead to their records, which are often substantial and filled with details of ships and destinations, and can contain personal details.

In the case of captains and officers, it will also include details of accidents, wrecks and enemy action. In some cases, where service at sea has been long there can be literally dozens of vessels and a world of visiting experience.

Information can also be gained at a local level. Trade directories, for example, tended to list local master mariners and their addresses (see the

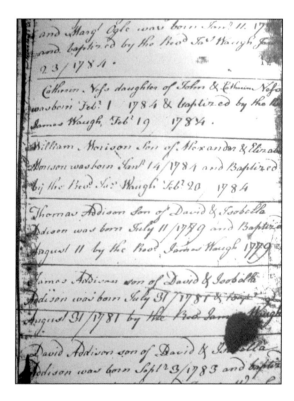

Details of seamen applying to enter maritime homes in the nineteenth century.

Research Guide). In the 1856 trade directory for Maryport over ninety master mariners were recorded, many living close to each other.

The Local Studies Library in Sunderland on Wearside has copies of the remarkable Trafalgar Square Papers.

These are invaluable to anyone fortunate enough to have ancestors who lived in the sailors' homes in the Square or applied to do so. From the 1840s the homes provided accommodation in 104 separate units for ex-seamen able to prove strong Wearside connections. Each unit was capable of taking a man and wife, a widow or a widower. In many cases, the records of applicants are incredibly detailed.

In May 1852, for example, Richard Burnikell applied for assistance on account of his age. He was aged sixty-nine, five-foot seven and seven-eighths tall (not five-foot eight, note!). His hair was described as 'white and bald' and he had grey eyes and a fair complexion. He was born in Staithes, Yorkshire and had married Elizabeth Nicholson at St Hilda's Church, South Shields on 27 September 1821. In 1852, he was living at Nicholson Street, Bishopwearmouth, and the dates and details of all the vessels on which he served were provided. He was given a pension of £3-8-0 a year; all excellent biographical detail.

Details of accidents and voyages can be followed up in local papers and, in some cases, fortune may have provided the family with material, as in the case of the descendants of Captain Joseph Scrafton of Sunderland. Scrafton captained a small sailing ship called the *Mary Ada* in the 1860s and 1870s and all letters received from the ship's agents, details of goods and journey have survived to allow us a wonderful insight into the life of a Victorian sea captain.

The records of actual shipping companies may also prove useful.

The Whitehaven office of the Cumbrian Archives has a few such documents among the Curwen papers, and the Carlisle office keeps a fascinating set of eighteenth-century records relating to the shipping of coal from Maryport; in these documents both masters and vessels are named.

The Barrow records deal mainly with shipbuilding but also relate to some trade carried out from the iron-ore mines at Millom. Here again relevant vessels are named.

The Tyne and Wear Archives has material concerning shipping on both Tyneside and Wearside. In relation to the Tyne, there are records affecting companies such as Hall Bros, Common Bros and the North Shields Stag Line, plus official documents on the operation of shipping on the river (pilots and maintenance).

In relation to Wearside shipping, the same archives has maritime trade and navigation records for steamship companies such as the Argosy Steamship Company (1882–1922) and Westoll's. There are also port authority records for the Wear. On occasions, these records can include references to officers and apprentices.

Also on Tyneside, the local studies section at South Tyneside Library in South Shields has photographs related to shipping.

The Teesside Archives has a large number of records relating to the Tyne Tees Shipping Company. These commence in the middle of the nineteenth century. Documents concerning customs and excise activity around the Hartlepools, Middlesbrough and Stockton also exist from the beginning of Victoria's reign.

As far as river workers are concerned, the Tyne and Wear Archives has records for a number of professional and employers' associations related to working on the river. It also keeps papers concerning the coal industry that include lists of keelmen and accounts of interviews. Records here stretch back into the seventeenth century.

Flesh on the Bones

Transport is well served by the museums and heritage centres of the North Country and it is fairly easy to build up a picture of any ancestral involvement in this field.

In Cumbria both the Helena Thompson Museum in Workington and the Dock Museum in Barrow-in-Furness have material relating to railways and railway development as well as the local harbours and docks.

In Northumberland the Bailiffgate Museum in Alnwick features its local railway, and on Tyneside the Stephenson Railway Museum can be found in the appropriately named Middle Engine Lane in North Shields. On display here is George Stephenson's *Puffing Billy*, a forerunner of his more famous *Rocket*, and there is detailed information on the building of railway engines. Here too is a display entitled 'From Pits to Staiths', which will be of special interest to those with ancestors involved in the transport of coal.

The Bowes Railway, although postmarked Gateshead, lies just within the southern boundaries of South Tyneside. Originally a colliery railway built to carry coal, mainly from pits in north-west Durham to the Tyne at Jarrow, its earliest section was the work of George Stephenson. It started operations in 1826, as one of the world's first modern railways, and is the only working preserved standard-gauge rope-hauled railway in the world.

Monkwearmouth Station Museum on Wearside has been in operation since the station closed as a working station in the late-twentieth century, and has recently enjoyed another closure for extensive refurbishment. The museum is now dedicated to social aspects of transport history and covers many different forms of transport.

In its heyday, Monkwearmouth was Sunderland's main station from Scotland and the North, a role it lost when a railway bridge enabled passengers to cross the river by train. It then enjoyed another period of prosperity as the main alighting point for holidaymakers bound for day trips or longer holidays at the popular resorts of Seaburn and Roker, which lay a short bus ride away.

In Modern County Durham, Beamish Museum displays a local wagon way and railway station, and the Tanfield Railway, near the market-town of Stanley, is the oldest existing 'railway' in the world. Its track was first laid in 1725 and wagons were drawn by horses and pulled along wooden rails. This railway witnessed the development of transport through stationary engines to the locomotive and still operates steam trains today along a three-mile stretch. Tanfield also keeps a collection of locomotives and carriages, and has a vintage workshop in an old engine shed.

Nearby Causey Arch is claimed to be the oldest surviving railway bridge in the world and was depicted on the late-twentieth-century Stephenson £5 note. The bridge can be visited and crossed throughout the year. It stands twenty-four metres high and was used by horse-drawn coal transport heading towards the Tyne.

The Weardale Railway also operates from time to time from Wolsingham to Stanhope. This is a new venture – five miles of track, which also sees the running of steam trains.

The National Railway Museum at Shildon is now one of the country's chief railway museums. It celebrates the history of one of the world's oldest railway towns and is the first national museum in the North-East.

Timothy Hackworth, Superintendent of the Stockton and Darlington Railway, set his engine works up here in the early-nineteenth century. The first passenger train on the first passenger railway left from Shildon in 1825. The museum is based around Hackworth's house and works, and features around sixty vehicles along with a replica of *Locomotion*. Engine sheds can be visited and short rides taken along a stretch of the original Stockton and Darlington Railway. An earlier museum was dedicated to the railway pioneer himself but became part of this wider national railway museum complex early in the twenty-first century.

In the Tees Valley, the Museum of Hartlepool has displays showing the importance of railway development to the twin towns of Hartlepool and West Hartlepool, and the Darlington Railway Centre and Museum aims to recreate the atmosphere of the steam age. It deals with the site of North Road Station as it was in 1842, has many railway relics and is situated in a set of very early railway buildings.

The newly refurbished Dorman Museum also deals with aspects of Middlesbrough's important links with the early railway.

Shipping is equally well represented. In Cumbria, Maryport celebrates its Georgian roots with a museum which concentrates on maritime history. Sited at the point of the port's earliest development, it displays material relating to local man Fletcher Christian and the mutiny on the *Bounty* and also to Thomas Ismay, owner of the *Titanic*. There are also good displays of maritime-related objects.

Whitehaven boasts a Georgian harbour and thrives on nostalgia. Slaves, sailors and rich merchants all come into the equation here. The Rum Story, opened at the Millenium, contains material of interest to those with ancestors on the West Cumbrian coast and also deals with trade at the Caribbean end.

The Dock Museum at Barrow-in-Furness straddles a Victorian graving dock and deals with aspects of shipping as well as shipbuilding.

The Story of the Tyne gallery at Newcastle's Discovery Museum examines many aspects of shipping and trade, and Souter Lighthouse, on the coast, will be of interest to those with ancestors in the maritime coastal service. Souter was the first lighthouse in the world specifically constructed for electric illumination by carbon arc lamps. Today it is possible to visit the Victorian keeper's cottage and the engine room.

Wearside shipping features in some of the displays in Sunderland Museum and Art Gallery, and the Museum of Hartlepool (and its excellent website) tells the story of the building of harbours and docks in the twin towns of Hartlepool and 'West'.

A number of sites around the Tees Valley deal with the life and deeds of that great Yorkshire sailor, discoverer and adventurer Captain James Cook (see the Yorkshire volume in this series).

For those with ancestors who worked on the river, The Story of the Tyne gallery at Newcastle's Discovery Museum has a display on the keelmen.

A summer boat trip from the Quay to the river-mouth can also be valuable in assessing the wide range of activities that used to take place on the river.

In Stockton, both museums – Preston Hall and The Green Dragon – have links with different forms of transport. The building that houses the latter was once on a major trading route and lies close to the line of the famed Stockton and Darlington Railway.

There are of course other forms of transport that deserve consideration – in particular, civilian aviation, buses and trams. They are not covered in this work, but interested researchers will be able to find adequate helpful literature, about buses and trams in particular, and will find a visit to the North of England Open Air Museum at Beamish very useful.

Chapter Six

OTHER INDUSTRIES

Although many of our North Country ancestors came to be employed in mining, shipbuilding, iron and steel manufacture and agriculture, the region also supported other significant industries. Space does not allow for reference to all of these in great detail yet commercial fishing, cloth production, pottery, glass and chemicals, in particular, are worthy of more than a passing reference.

Commercial fishing has a lengthy history on both coasts. On the west coast, local families owned many of the fishing vessels, and fleets from Scotland and Ireland visited its ports and harbours during the herring season.

In the north of Cumbria and nearby southern Scotland, the Solway coast between Carlisle and Bowness was home to exponents of the haaf-net system.

In the east, there were few major ports that did not have a fish quay, and many coastal villages, such as Seahouses, Craster, Amble, Alnmouth, Beadnell and Newbiggin-by-the-Sea, in Northumberland, plus Cullercoats and North Shields, on Tyneside, enjoyed reputations for the quality and quantity of their catches.

All kinds of fish were caught, including cod, halibut, plaice and ling. Most important of all, perhaps, was the seasonal herring trade, which caused considerable movement of the population, who were chasing after the 'shoals of herring'. This trade may help to explain relationships and marriages which took place up and down the east coast: a number of researchers in the North-East will be able to trace ancestry to the area around Kings Lynn.

The North-East again became well known for its fishermen and 'fishlasses'. The nineteenth-century historian of Hartlepool, Cuthbert Sharp, included pictures of them and their equipment in his history of the old town.

'Old' Hartlepool was a significant fishing port for many years. As rival town West Hartlepool developed, the fishermen of the old town became the butt of witty tales, including the infamous tale of the 'hanging' of a monkey as a spy during the Napoleonic Wars.

Women were involved in the fishing business at many points, baiting the

The fishermen of Hartlepool - butt of a local legend.

lines, cleaning, gutting and selling the fish, and also in knitting the famous fisherman's jerseys, or ganseys, and weaving the special baskets or creels.

The fishwives often took their wares inland and many of them became well-known local characters. Thus we have the famed Cullercoats fish lass, celebrated in a Victorian music hall song, and Meg Shipley, the twentieth-century crab lady from Sunderland.

Glass Making was another industry which operated on both coasts. From the middle of the eighteenth century, Maryport was associated with the glass trade when Lancelot Atkinson of Newcastle upon Tyne and Penrith wine merchant George Monkhouse set up a glassworks there. This business declined in the late-eighteenth century and was gone before the end of the Napoleonic Wars.

Glass was also produced on the banks of the Tyne. Glass workers (Lorrainers) settled here in the late-medieval period, driven out of their homes by religious disputes.

The proximity of coalfields was an important factor in the development of the glass industry around the Tyne and Wear and in the mid-nineteenth century firms such as Cookson's of South Shields were well known for the production of window glass.

The choice of the banks of the Wear at Sunderland as the site of the modern National Glass Centre is an apt one; the Wearside has strong and enduring links with glass making. Both Pyrex and Hartley's, names well known in the glass world, had works here (Hartley won a huge contract for the production of glass for the Crystal Palace in 1851).

Although the jobs in the industry were diverse, workers often co-operated in family groups. In the early-nineteenth century there were some thirty glass-producing firms on Tyneside alone making bottle, sheet and window glass. In 1868, the Tyne Plate Glass Company employed some 600 workers.

Glassworkers and their masters turn up in all the usual genealogical records, from seventeen-year-old Sunderland girl Mary Dalton (described as a 'glass worker' in the 1871 census), to Walter Horn, residing in The Elms, a 'glass manu-facturer' in 1881. He was born *c*.1849 at North Hylton right beside the River Wear. Not all workers were simply described as such and may also appear as glass makers, cutters, blowers or even engravers.

Cloth production never became the real force it was elsewhere in the North of England during the industrial revolution, although there were significant pockets of activity throughout the region, and the domestic system relating to wool could be found in a number of rural areas. In a county famed for its sheep, it is hardly surprising to find wool in various guises 'part of the whole fabric' and that this, in turn, led to the production of other forms of cloth.

As early as the fourteenth century, Flemish workers settled into the cloth trade in Kendal, a town which still has as its motto the words *Panus Mihi Panis* – 'Wool is My Bread'. Kendal cottons were also well known in the eighteenth century and the product of spinners went to weavers all over the country and, in particular, to Norfolk and London.

Cloth production was marked in and around Sedbergh on the Yorkshire –Westmorland border. The poet Southey wrote an interesting and amusing tale about 'terrible knitters of Dent' in the southernmost tip of the region. These knitters had a fearsome reputation for the ferocity of their work rate; the lime-stone riverbeds where much of the cleansing of wool and cloth was carried out can still be visited here and the old cloth trade routes followed on foot.

During the same period, the agriculturist Arthur Young noted that in Cumberland and Westmorland, farmers' wives spun and took wool to market every week.

Ivy Pinchbeck, in her well-researched book on working women, refers to one Cumbrian spinner in the late-eighteenth century who went out spinning wool for her neighbours fifteen weeks in the year; the rest of the year she spun lint at home for a manufacturer. She also did some reaping at harvest time.

Carlisle was one of the centres for fabrics and the Ferguson family were particularly well known. Dixon's Chimney, part of a large cloth mill, remains a Cumbrian landmark today. Robert Anderson, the Cumberland Bard, was a cloth printer in the city during the time of the Napoleonic Wars and a later writer, W T Johnston, also worked in the trade.

The Cumbrian poets and songwriters of this period make numerous ref-erences to spinning and weaving. The eighteenth-century Cumbrian poet

Textile washing area – Dent.

Susanna Blamire wrote a song which looked at life from behind a spinning wheel. Anderson refers to the weavers of Whorton on a number of occasions and heralded the real-life marriage of a weaver in his song 'The Caldbeck Wedding'. The song, which stretches to over twenty verses in length, tells of the marriage of Joseph Bewley and Mary Dalton, which is registered in the parish record as having taken place on Christmas Day 1804.

Dyers and fullers were also found in Durham in medieval times and there were pockets of large-scale tailoring in the Durham and Wearside areas in the late-twentieth century.

Perhaps one of the most significant cloth areas in the region lay in and around Darlington, which flourished with the weaving and dyeing of cloth from medieval times and developed industries connected to leather and linen in the years leading up to the industrial revolution. Much of this was due to Darlington's key geographical position on the main eastern road route between London and Edinburgh.

The **pottery** industry also has links with the region, and examples from the banks of the Tyne and the Wear can be found in the museums around the world. One name readily associated with North-Eastern pottery is that of Maling. The Malings had produced pottery on Wearside in the eighteenth century but Christopher Thompson Maling (1824–91) established the firm as a real force on Tyneside. Maling succeeded at many different levels, from jam pots to pieces of true elegance, and is probably most famous for its links with the Rington Tea Company. Of significance to genealogists here is the number of workers who, according to histories of the firm, left the Staffordshire potteries to work for Maling in the North-East.

Sunderland pottery enjoyed enormous popularity and remains collectible and, in some cases, useful to the family historian through its tendency to specialise in named memorial pieces (see Flesh on the Bones below).

The **chemical industry**, often regarded as a modern one, is in fact an industry with deep roots. Salt production took place across the region for centuries (in Billingham, for example, since the fourteenth century). In the early days the process was simple, and combined solar evaporation with boiling, using small coal as the fuel.

Prior to the 1880s there were chemical works on the south banks of the Tyne at Gateshead, Jarrow and Hebburn. In the middle of the century, over 3,000 people in the Tyne area were employed in the industry and one eminent historian notes that, along with Merseyside, Tyneside 'dominated the British chemical industry'.

These works were eventually abandoned in favour of developments around the Tees. One of the earliest works established there was in 1833 at Urlay Nook, just west of Yarm. This came in the shape of the Egglescliffe Chemical Company. Other discoveries of salt took the industry further in that direction and, in the years before the First World War, there were a number of companies such as Bell Bros, Pease and Partners, The Cleveland Salt Company and United Alkali Company around the Tees Valley.

Worried by the prospect of lost imports during the First World War, the government bought a site at Billingham-on-Tees where anhydrite and salt and were both available for nitrates. Slightly later, this complex developed into Imperial Chemical Industries Limited (ICI) and moved into the production of fertilisers and synthetics. ICI has been a household name and a great employer around the Tees ever since. As the years passed, the firm simply diversified into new product including methanol, oil tar, creosote and perspex. Later still came British Oxygen and British Titan, and even today, the Tees Plain resembles a giant chemistry set when viewed from the surrounding heights.

Another of the region's industries is energy production, and specifically, **nuclear energy**. In the second half of the twentieth century this industry too was a big employer, in West Cumbria in particular, with the names of Windscale (Sellafield) and Calder Hall well known. Ever controversial, the industry has been regarded as a valuable employer by many in the area. There is also a nuclear power station near Hartlepool.

Cumbrian ancestors also became increasingly involved in the **tourism industry**. With the work of the Lakeland poets in the early-nineteenth century,

Early tourism in Lakeland.

and of various artists over the years, then, ultimately, the opening of the railway, the Lake District became a haven for both short- and long-stay holidaymakers.

The attraction of the Lakes was its variety from season to season, which was captured well in the words of Robert Anderson:

> *There's ULLSWATER, BASSENTHWAITE, WASTWATER, DERWENT*
> *That thousands on thousands have travell'd to view.*
> *The longer they gaze, still the more they may wonder*
> *And, aye as they wonder may find 'summet' new*

The ever-changing beauty of the Lakes meant good business for shopkeepers, hoteliers, bed-and-breakfast operators and providers of climbing equipment, to name a few. Steam cruising also became popular on the lakes at Ullswater, Windermere and Coniston.

By the late-twentieth century, many other areas in the region (including Northumberland and the entire Pennine area) had developed flourishing tourist trades.

Finding More

With such a diverse set of industries, it is possible to give only a few examples and some basic advice about discovering more about ancestors. Generally the entry of key words into online sites can prove helpful here and save fruitless visits.

As regards fishing/fisherman/fisheries, much of the archival material available deals with rights to the sport of fishing. However, solicitors' papers in both the Barrow and Kendal offices of the Cumbrian Archives do mention named professional fishermen, and the Carlisle records are extensive for fishermen earning a living around the margins of the Solway.

Records in the Northumbrian Archives often relate to fisheries on the River Tweed but there are also references to fishermen in the Morpeth Asylum and some oral recordings of fishermen made in the late-twentieth century.

The Tyne and Wear Archives keeps useful records relating to the registration and crewing of fishing boats at North Shields.

The magnificent Northumberland Communities website also deals in detail with the history and workings of many of the Northumberland fishing communities (see appendix 2, Web Resources).

The Tyne and Wear Archives has interesting material both online and in store in connection with the Hartley Brothers Glass Manufactory in Sunderland and Cookson's in South Shields. In the latter case, letter books have survived and there are scrapbooks and photographs in the Hartley files.

Keying 'Cotton', 'Calico' and 'Wool' brings to light useful evidence in Cumbria. The Kendal Archives, for example, has the papers of Braithwaite's Woollen Manufacturers in Kendal and these include wages books for the nineteenth century. The Carlisle office has records relating to local calico and cotton production.

In connection with the chemical industry, the Whitehaven office of the Cumbria Archives has material relating to the Harrington Chemical Works. The Tyne and Wear Archives has surveyors' papers which cover a number of chemical factories along the Tyne, including the works at Felling, Heworth and Friar's Goose in the mid-nineteenth century.

Teesside Archive papers relate mostly to the late-twentieth century but there is some early material on the establishment of chemical works in Middlesbrough.

Flesh on the Bones

Many of the 'other industries' featured in the chapter have areas in museums and heritage centres dedicated to them.

Maryport features the fishing industry in a number of displays. A walk around the paved area of the Elizabethan dock there will prove enlightening about the role of the commercial fishing fleet.

The Helena Thompson Museum at Workington deals with the early fishing industry around Workington and Harrington.

The 'Story of the Tyne' gallery at Newcastle's Discovery Museum has a case dedicated to the story of the fishing industry and there are various references throughout the gallery to the important Fish Quay at North Shields.

Further south, the award-winning Saltburn Smugglers Centre is set in ancient fishermen's cottages. The centre combines costumed characters with authentic sounds and smells and serves as a reminder that not all our fishing ancestors spent their time on the right side of the law.

The Discovery Museum also displays memorabilia from the glassmaking industry but a day in Sunderland is probably more fruitful for those with family who were involved with glass. The National Glass Centre here deals with the general history of the industry, and Sunderland Museum and Art Gallery houses a number of interesting displays. One is dedicated to objects made by glassmakers for fun out of pieces of left-over glass.

The Museum of Lakeland Life in Kendal keeps artefacts connected to the cloth trade. Further south in the former Yorkshire area of Cumbria, Farfield Mill at Sedbergh has evidence useful for tracing the history of the wool industry in the area. The special accent here is on spinning, weaving and old machinery.

As a bobbin mill, Stott Park Mill, near Lake Windermere, was also involved in the cloth trade.

Some examples of local Cumbrian pottery can be found at the Helena Thompson Museum in Workington.

In Sunderland, the popular pottery gallery at Sunderland Museum and Art Gallery may be of special interest to some family historians as local potteries (which include the early Maling) specialised in the production of christening, wedding and memorial ware. It is often possible to trace the original purchasers of these through the usual genealogical research routes and at least a dozen named people have so far been found on the census, in parish registers or civil registration.

The saddest memorial here comes in the shape of a couple of pots dedicated to Monica Evelyn Dolan (dated 18 May 1881) and Elizabeth Dolan (dated 5 February 1879). From the census it becomes obvious that these were christening mugs; the death registers show little Monica's death in the March quarter of 1882. Interestingly, not all those involved in commissioning these pots came from the wealthier classes.

In the museums along the West Cumbrian coast there are displays, some permanent and others temporary, relating to the influence of the chemical and nuclear industries. Keswick Museum traces the development of the town from mining centre to tourist centre.

In Tees Valley, Middlesbrough's Dorman Museum has photographs relating to general industries around the Tees. The Preston Hall and Green Dragon museums at Stockton both host displays connected to a number of local industries.

Section Two

NORTH COUNTRY LIFE

Chapter Seven

RELIGION

Even before the period generally regarded by family historians as 'recorded time', North Country folk were heavily involved in religious matters. In Roman times, soldiers serving on the Wall worshipped the Persian god Mithras. During the period of the Saxon kingdoms, Christian kings met non-Christians in fierce conflict, and Saxon saints such as Cuthbert, Bede and Benedict Biscop were at the forefront of the development of Christianity.

Great decisions marking the breakaway of Roman Christianity from the Celtic form were made in the region, and Lindisfarne, or Holy Island, famed for its gospels, remains a place of pilgrimage today. After the Norman Conquest there were further significant developments, with the construction of great buildings such as Durham Cathedral, where the remains of two northern saints, Bede and Cuthbert, lie buried.

The passage of the bishopric of Durham into history as 'the land of the Prince Bishops' speaks volumes about the power and influence of the Church in the

Modern County Durham recalls its past.

St Peter's, Monkwearmouth – home to Bede and Biscop.

region during medieval times; this power was to decline with the Reformation of the Church in the sixteenth century.

Above all, religion became the major guardian of records useful to the study of family history, at least from the sixteenth century to the beginning of civil registration in the early- to mid-nineteenth century. Details of these records are dealt with in this chapter, making it of particular interest to researchers keen to trace their family tree further back towards Tudor times.

The Main Religions

The Church of England had problems in establishing itself in the region during the early days of the Reformation when there were two major risings in defence of 'the Old Faith'. In the eighteenth century, the Stuarts involved in the Jacobite uprising were hoping for widespread support from Catholics within the region but they were to be disappointed; by the eighteenth century attitudes had clearly changed.

Thus the parish church established itself as the centre of the community – a place of government and administration as well as a centre for faith with its wider organisation recording not merely baptisms, marriages and burials but also details of tithe collection plus wills and inventories where applicable (see Finding More below and chapter 9, Local Government).

The organisation of the Church of England in the region can appear quite complex at times. Generally speaking, the dioceses of interest for ancestral research here consist of Durham, Newcastle, York, Ripon and Leeds, in the North-East. In the North-West Cumbria consists mainly of the diocese of Carlisle with one or two parishes in the dioceses of Newcastle and Bradford.

Despite the strength of the established church, there were still strong pockets of Catholicism throughout the North Country, especially in those areas settled by Irish labourers, who came to build the harbours and the railways. In the Hartlepools in the 1860s, for example, there was a tussle over religion among the poor-law authorities, who were unhappy at having a priest visiting workhouse inmates. The priest in his defence noted that, in his area, which covered a large swathe of territory north of the Tees, he 'represented over a third of the people in religion'. Although Catholicism was not set up as an established hierarchy until the middle of the nineteenth century, there were missions and there is written evidence for Catholic activity in most parts of the North Country, some of it stretching back into the eighteenth century.

Methodism, with its simple appeal to the worker, enjoyed enormous popularity throughout the region. In some places the miners who had made the journey up from Devon and Cornwall brought the faith with them.When Cornish-born Jane Stephens died in West Cumbria in 1929, she was described in the local press as 'an old Millom Wesleyan' – her Devon-born late husband as 'a prominent Wesleyan'.

As with a number of the nonconformist religions, a major attraction of Methodism was the hope that good deeds and sober living would bring a better afterlife than the current one. John Wesley preached in the region on numerous occasions and his influence on the mining communities was considerable. A brief history of Durham and the Tees area, published in the 1970s, claims that he had 'more influence on religious thought in Durham than anyone else'. He was not always made welcome, however, and encountered considerable hostility in Newcastle.

The influence of Methodism was also to be seen in Trades Union activity in the region in the nineteenth century and, as elsewhere, with the passage of time Methodism itself became divided into smaller groups such as the New Connection Methodists and Primitive Methodists.

So widespread was Methodism that it seems inappropriate to highlight one part of the region yet Weardale, perhaps, deserves a specific mention. John Wesley visited there in 1752 and 1761, and High House Chapel, which opened its door in 1760, is still in operation today.

Another religion that found favour in the region was the Society of Friends. George Fox, founder of the Quakers, came to Westmorland in the seventeenth century and discovered quite a following in and close to the county. Brigflatts Quaker Meeting-house near Sedbergh dates from 1675 and is the oldest meeting-house in the north of England. The Friends' Meeting-house at Swarthmoor Hall in the Furness area was built by Fox himself in 1688 after he came into possession of it as a result of his marriage to the widow of Judge Fell.

One of the Quaker Fell family, William Fell, who was born at nearby Trinkeld in 1697, made a considerable contribution to American history as the founder of the first shipbuilding industry in Baltimore. The old part of Baltimore is still known as Fell's Point; it is central to local heritage trails, and the work of the Fell family is readily acknowledged and celebrated in the city.

In the north of Cumbria, a considerable congregation existed at Moorhouse on the Solway. At one point local men Thomas Stordy and David Hodgson suffered for their faith as Quakers. Neither man believed in the 'unchristian yoke of tithes' which they refused to both pay and receive, leading to frequent brushes with the law.

One urban area strongly linked to the Friends is Darlington, which embraced the Quaker ethics of sobriety and hard work. (Even today the nickname 'Quakers' has stuck with the local professional football team.) Famous Quaker families such as the Backhouses and Peases were closely involved with the Stockton and Darlington Railway and were also active in banking, ironstone mining and the linen and wool industries. They were also influential in political life, both locally and nationally.

The history of the Presbyterians, Congregationalists and Unitarians is not always easy to unravel. The Congregationalists, or Independents, did not agree with state interference with religion. Some of these with an interest in science and reason became involved in the Unitarian movement in the eighteenth and nineteenth centuries. Out of this too came the United Reform Church of the late-twentieth century.

One of the leaflets relating to the Berwick-upon-Tweed office of the Northumberland Archives notes that 'Presbyterianism was very strong in North Northumberland because of its proximity to Scotland: in the Berwick area it was stronger than the Established Church.'

As it was illegal before 1837 to marry in a nonconformist church (except for Jews and Quakers) it can be difficult to find records of the marriages of some of those who practised non-conformity just south of border. At times they chose to go north (famously to Gretna Green) but also to Coldstream and other places just across the border, where they felt the ceremony was more appropriate to their faith.

Many of the Shetland-born Pottingers, who appear from time to time in this book, can be found in the records of St George's Presbyterian Church in Sunderland, and Scottish-born shipowners, shipbuilders and master mariners throughout the region supported similar churches.

The history of the Baptist movement is also a complex one, dating in its organisation back to the Reformation and the early-seventeenth century. Traditionally Baptists have no creed and believe that all authority stems from the Bible. Common characteristics include baptism of mature adults rather than children, baptism via full immersion, the independence of local churches, and religious revivals.

The preacher as poet – Thomas Gregg from Millom and Coniston.

Surviving records suggest that the Baptist faith enjoyed some support in the region. Coniston-born miner, poet and mason Thomas Gregg was also a Baptist preacher and later helped to cement his faith by building a church in the Millom area. The strength of Gregg's faith can be gauged from his surviving poems and sermons. Although frightened by the possibility of being left outside God's Grace, he held a firm belief in the prospect of a wonderful afterlife and the hope of better things to come.

Further up the coast at Maryport, the Hine family showed an ardent commitment to the Baptist faith. Their Holme Shipping Line was an essential part of the local economy.

The relative decline in support for formal Christian religion in recent years should not blind us to its importance to our ancestors. In the nineteenth century, it was also linked to the anti-alcohol teetotal movement. One supporter of this movement was Mark Swaddle, a winding engineer at Washington F Pit and leader in his chapel; he kept a note in his diary of all the local crimes and unexpected deaths related to 'strong drink'; often he would note, soberly, 'drink did it'.

The Tyneside Bard, Joe Wilson, who kept a pub at one time, later turned teetotal and wrote many teetotal songs. This verse was sung to the old Folk tune 'Early in the Morning':

> *Shun vile intoxication!*
> *Keep from intoxication!*
> *It's vile intoxication!*
> *Makes the world so full of care!*

Many immigrants from Eastern Europe also brought the Hebrew faith with them (see chapter 14, Movement). Gateshead, Newcastle and Sunderland were important centres here and a fine synagogue and meeting-house, now abandoned, can still be seen beside the road leading from Sunderland to Ryhope.

Finding More

The twentieth-century movement of local government boundaries seems to have created more complications with the archiving of religious records than with many other forms of historic material. On a more positive note, the recent upsurge of interest in genealogy has ensured that copies of religious records, often regional as well as local, can be found in many of the major archive and local study centres throughout the region.

The Northumberland Archives Service, for example, has material relating to religious records in virtually every ancient North Country county touched on in this book, so you may save yourself some unnecessary travel by checking what religious records are available when researching at any of the region's centres.

As in other areas of the country, the existence of records of this nature depends on a combination of the thoroughness of clerks down the years and the circumstances of survival. Good fortune in both cases could carry a family history back to the reign of Henry VIII and the early-sixteenth century.

It is also worth pointing out that such is the mass of records available that no general attempt has been made in this chapter to differentiate between original copies, microfilm copies and printed copies. When used appropriately, archival guide sheets and websites will be useful guides here.

In relation to the church records for Cumbria, all four Cumbria Record Offices hold the standard ones for their area, such as the church registers from a wide number of Church of England and nonconformist churches.

Prior to 1858, probate in Cumbria was the responsibility of the Church of England, and wills and inventories relevant to the modern county came under the dioceses of Carlisle and Chester.

The Carlisle office holds the archives of the Diocese of Carlisle and Dean and

Chapter of Carlisle Cathedral. There are also probate records at Kendal covering the Deaneries of Kendal and Furness, and Carlisle. Probate records covering the Deanery of Copeland from 1466 to 1860 are kept at Whitehaven.

Tithe books for Penrith in the early-nineteenth century give the name of payer, crop, where growing, tithe sum, sum paid and other information; these can be found at the Carlisle office.

Among the material in the Tyne and Wear Archives are transcripts and indexes for eighteenth- and nineteenth-century Cumbrian marriages at St Augustine's Alston and parish records for St John Garigill for the same period.

The Northumberland County Archives has a wide range of religious records connected to Northumberland. There is solid Church of England material relating to Chillingham and Lesbury and registers relating to the Catholic faith as practised in Alnwick and at Whittingham St Mary.

The Methodist material here is very full, relating to all the Northumberland circuits, with some records going back to the middle of the eighteenth century.

This office also holds material for Presbyterianism in the Morpeth area.

Berwick-upon-Tweed Record Office keeps material relating mainly to North Northumberland. Here can be found a number of Anglican parish records on microfilm.

Presbyterianism was very strong in this area and this office possesses records for a number of relevant churches. Methodist records for the Berwick-upon-Tweed and Lowick circuit are also here and consist of baptism registers from the early-nineteenth century through to the early-twentieth century.

Catholic registers for Berwick survive from the early-nineteenth century and also transcripts of registers from Haggerston, Lowick and Wooler.

Blyth Local Studies Library has a list of monumental inscriptions from nearby Northumbrian churches. Hexham Library keeps transcriptions of parish registers for the Tynedale area

With the enormous historical links between Newcastle and Northumberland, it is natural that many Northumbrian records or copies of records can be viewed in the Tyne and Wear Archives. These include some Anglican parish records on microfilm (Lowick from the eighteenth century and Ponteland from the seventeenth century for example) and Quaker records for Allendale from the nineteenth century as well as tithe maps for Northumberland.

There are also a number of Northumbrian Catholic records here including early-nineteenth-century records for Felton and late-nineteenth-century ones for Haydon Bridge.

The Durham County Record Office also holds the records of the Durham and Northumberland Congregational Union, which include Alnwick baptisms, marriages and burials for the late-nineteenth century/early-twentieth century.

Many of the relevant Tyneside church records can be found at the Tyne and Wear Archives where microfilm copies of the Church of England registers are kept. Those of St Hilda's at South Shields go back to the seventeenth century and those of St Mary's, Gateshead to the sixteenth century.

There are also registers relating to the various branches of Methodism. Circuits include Blaydon and Gateshead, Jarrow, North and South Shields as well as individual churches across Tyneside.

There are also records of other denominations – eighteenth-century Baptist records from North Shields and seventeenth-century Quaker records for Newcastle plus documents from the groups that were to join forces eventually as the United Reform Church.

There are Catholic records for Tyneside too, some stretching back into the eighteenth century, and extensive records of Jewish communities, which were especially active in Newcastle and Gateshead.

At Gateshead Central Library, material kept includes some Tyneside parish records.

The local studies section at South Tyneside Library in South Shields has Church of England records, and the local studies collection in North Tyneside Central Library in North Shields has some limited Anglican parish registers. There are microfilm copies here of registers from the parish churches of Killingworth, Longbenton, Tynemouth Christ Church and Tynemouth Holy Trinity.

Many church records for Tyneside can be viewed at the Durham County Record Office, where there is Church of England material relating to Gateshead, Jarrow and Boldon from the sixteenth century as well as Felling, Hebburn, Heworth and South Shields.

South Shields has Baptist, Presbyterian and Congregational records here. There are also Congregational records for East Boldon and Felling, and Presbyterian records for Gateshead, as well as Roman Catholic material for Newcastle and South Shields.

Northumberland County Record Office also has copies of Presbyterian records and some Congregational records for parts of Tyneside.

With the area within the bounds of the City of Sunderland formerly in the Historic County of Durham, it is no surprise to discover many relevant Wearside records still in the Durham County Record Office. These include those relating to Church of England parishes in Bishopwearmouth, Houghton-le-Spring, Monkwearmouth, Sunderland and Washington plus Methodist material for Bishopwearmouth, Houghton and Sunderland.

Roman Catholic records also relate to St Mary's Chapel in Bishopwearmouth during the very-early-nineteenth century.

The Durham office also has a number of Wearside Congregational, Presbyterian and Quaker documents.

There are no original Church of England registers at the Tyne and Wear Archives relating to Wearside but there are a large number on microfilm, including baptisms, marriages and burials at Bishopwearmouth from the sixteenth century.

The guide to Methodist records here comes with a very clear summary of the history of the religion, pointing the way to material from Sunderland and district from the early-nineteenth century.

There are also a number of nonconformist records for Wearside at the Tyne and Wear Archives, some going back into the eighteenth century, including Baptist, German Lutheran, Unitarian, Congregational and Presbyterian. Catholic records have a separate user guide.

There is an extensive collection of Jewish material, some going back into the nineteenth century; also a copy of an interesting thesis on Jewish migration from Lithuania to Sunderland in the nineteenth and twentieth centuries.

The Local Studies Centre in Sunderland Central Library has copies of most of the Church of England records relating to Wearside 'as well as many Roman Catholic and nonconformist registers'.

The Corder Manuscripts (mentioned in chapter 2, Shipbuilding), are also useful to those studying Quaker families on Wearside.

The Durham County Record Office has key material relating to religious records in Modern County Durham. There are Church of England Records for most of the major parishes, and the range of Methodist records for the pit communities is an indicator of the regional popularity of this religion in its many different guises.

Seaham, for example, has left records for both the Colliery and the Harbour Wesleyan Methodist churches, a United Methodist Free Church and a number of primitive Methodist churches

There are a number of Presbyterian records here including those for Seaham Harbour, Benfieldside, Crook (St Andrew) and Claypath Presbyterian Chapel in Durham City itself.

Baptist records include those for Consett Front Street, Bishop Auckland, Cockton Hill and Spennymoor Church Street. There are also records for the Society of Friends.

The Tyne and Wear Archives also has material of use to those studying ancestry in Modern County Durham. A number of Church of England parish records can be seen on microfilm – Croxdale back into the seventeenth century and Sherburn Hospital the same, and a number of Catholic and nonconformist nineteenth century and twentieth century.

Catholic material here includes Birtley St Joseph's with baptism, marriage and burial transcripts for the Belgian refugee community at Elisabethville.

There are also records relating to wills and marriage bonds for Durham.

In relation to Tees Valley material, Teesside Archives has Church of England records for St Luke, Thornaby, Eston and Skelton in Cleveland plus Catholic records for Stockton, Hartlepool, West Hartlepool and Middlesbrough.

Here too there is a mass of material relating to Methodist circuits and in particular, those based on Hartlepool and Middlesborough plus a large number of Methodist marriage registers from the late-nineteenth century onwards.

There are also a few Presbyterian records here.

Many of the church records relating to the Tees Valley are still to be found at the Durham County Record Office. This applies particularly to those relating to Darlington, a town that has retained very close links with Modern County Durham.

Church of England material for Billingham, Darlington, Hartlepool and West Hartlepool, Redmarshall, Sadberge, Seaton Carew and Stockton are kept at Durham, as are some Roman Catholic records for Darlington, Hartlepool and Stockton.

The Durham office has material relating to Methodist, Wesleyan Methodist, and New Connexion, United and Primitive Methodist churches in Darlington and also some Methodist records for Hartlepool, West Hartlepool and Stockton.

There are also records for Congregational churches and chapels in both Darlington and Stockton, and for the Society of Friends in Darlington, Middlesbrough, Redcar, Saltburn, Stockton and West Hartlepool.

The Darlington Centre for Local Studies has records relating to Darlington and nearby places in both the Modern and Historic County of Durham. A complete list of relevant registers is available on the website. It also has some nonconformist, Roman Catholic and Quaker records as well as monumental inscriptions.

Tyne and Wear Archives has some Tees Valley Church of England records on microfilm, including those for Redmarshall back to the sixteenth century and Stockton St Thomas back to the seventeenth century. Boyd's Marriage Index for Durham 1538–1817, marriage bonds for the seventeenth and eighteenth centuries and an index to Durham wills for the late-eighteenth century may also be found here.

The Northumberland County Record Office also keeps copies of some records for Catholic Darlington from the eighteenth century onwards.

Flesh on the Bones

Although arguably of minimal relevance to the family historian, the region's ancient religious establishments are well worth a visit, if only to get a flavour of the religious region in ancient times. Sites include churches developed in Saxon times at Hart, near Hartlepool, and at Escomb, as well as the Saxon monastic sites at Monkwearmouth and Jarrow.

Those with roots in County Durham, Historic or Modern, must look around the magnificent cathedral in Durham City. Those with an interest in Carlisle should visit its cathedral, which has always played an important role in local life, and now houses a display relating to the history of Christianity in Cumbria.

The abbeys at Furness, Hexham and Shap, and on Holy Island, also have tales to tell.

Individual churches are worth seeking out where there is a family connection although many of the smaller nonconformist meeting places have changed function; in the colliery villages in the North-East, it is not unusual to find such buildings now used as garages, warehouses and even private houses.

In modern Hartlepool, both the Wesley Chapel and West Hartlepool's first important Anglican Church (in Church Square) have new functions, with the latter serving as a heritage centre. On the other hand, some religious establishments have gone up in the world: the parish church at Bishopwearmouth near the modern city centre of Sunderland has been afforded Minster status in recent times.

In Kendal, a number of heritage sites celebrate the town's links with the Society of Friends, while early Quaker history can be examined at nearby Mosedale.

In Northumberland, the parish church at Berwick, opened in 1652, is a unique Cromwellian church and its graveyard contains the remains of victims of the plague.

On Wearside, a family-history-friendly organisation has helped to save a defunct cemetery and its records. The cemetery is at Houghton-le-Spring and the organisation, which has a regularly maintained website, is called the Friends of Hillside Cemetery.

The cemetery opened in the mid-1850s as an outbreak of cholera hit the Sunderland area. Fearful that the existing graveyard would be too small, the vicar gained parliamentary permission to commence burials on the site of an old quarry. This proved an unpopular move with residents, who were unhappy at the positioning of the graveyard. Over the last half century, the cemetery has fallen into disrepair. Thanks to 'The Friends', things are now looking up and their website not only logs the history of the cemetery, which closed to burials in the late-twentieth century, but is also gradually recording the names and dates of burials there.

Up in Weardale, High House Chapel, linked to Wesley from the mid-eighteenth century, now hosts the Weardale Museum, which celebrates the religious and social history of the dale.

Graveyards linked to churches continue to keep their appeal; St Hilda's in Old Hartlepool, for example, has stones dedicated to Christopher Furness, founder of the local railway and Billy Purvis, the nineteenth-century comedian and entertainer.

Chapter Eight

NATIONAL GOVERNMENT

This could easily have been the longest chapter in the book. That it isn't stands as a tribute to the massive amount of material available nationally which deals with this extremely wide topic. It is at a national level too that much of the evidence related to the topic can be most readily studied.

Thus the chapter deals with local genealogical material connected to the machinery of national government. Such machinery controlled the taking of censuses, the developing of civil registration (effectively from the early years of the reign of Queen Victoria) and the recording of voting qualification. Up until the 1870s, this might also include written evidence for the way in which North Country ancestors actually voted.

The Material

The 1830s Act of Parliament which set up the compulsory collection of details on Births, Deaths and Marriages in England and Wales took a little while to bed in, but from the 1840s onwards, the records they produced are fairly accurate. Registration Districts were established throughout the region and, as elsewhere in the country, copies of the information gathered were kept both locally and nationally (see Finding More for further details).

The census existed as a statistical exercise from 1801, started to record individual information in 1841 and became fairly thorough from 1851 onwards. With a hundred-year secrecy rule in force, only those taken every ten years from 1841 to 1901 are currently in the public domain (although much work is being done to enable access to the 1911 census to take place at an earlier date).

As with civil registration, the work of local enumerators over the years can be viewed in various forms and at various places (see Finding More). Examples of entries from North Country censuses have been used throughout this book.

Much of the election-related material is kept only locally and deserves fuller coverage. As a rule of thumb, no females had the right to vote before the First World War, and very few men, prior to the 1860s. Northumberland's own Earl Grey was prime minister in 1832 when the so-called 'Great Reform Act' was passed, but comparatively few benefited, as the right to vote remained solidly based on extensive property-holding for some time after.

Voting for MPs was carried out in either county or borough constituencies. Up to 1832, those voting for an MP in a county constituency had to be male, over twenty-one, and in possession of freehold land that could be rented for forty shillings a year or more. The borough constituencies were a law unto themselves and varied from a single voter, in one notorious case, to the entire adult male population in another, and qualifications were extremely complex!

Up to 1832, and in many cases, 1867, many major towns and cities developed in the industrial revolution did not have their own MPs. As the century progressed, more males gained the vote and more urban areas were granted MPs. The 1867 Act had a particularly great effect on the political map of the North Country.

Details of the right to vote were recorded on an electoral roll and, up to the introduction of the secret ballot in the 1870s, details of the actual votes cast were supposed to be recorded in a poll book. If your North Country ancestor qualified for a vote, there is a chance that his details will turn up in such documents if they have survived.

Lists of electors may be found catalogued today as electoral rolls, lists of burgesses (in the case of boroughs) or simply lists of voters. Many were drawn up in the nineteenth and twentieth centuries and large numbers have survived. The names and addresses of voters were noted down and, in the days when property was vital, the address of the property or combined properties they owned that carried the vote.

The political experiences of two members of the seafaring Pottinger family may act as a useful guide to the type of information available here. In the mid-1860s, William and James Pottinger were young married master mariners living in Sunderland, which had become a borough for elections under the 1832 Act. Neither man had the vote prior to 1867. Both were enfranchised as a result of the 1867 Act and appear in the electoral rolls for the rest of their lives. They gained their vote based on ownership of more than one property. These properties are listed as well as their home addresses, providing useful extra information about their economic status.

Poll books recording votes cast were often printed and sold locally after the elections. There was a legal requirement to do this from the late-eighteenth century and poll books existed until a secret ballot was introduced in 1872. These books usually contain the name of the community in which the voter lived, the name of the community where he owned the property that gave him the vote, what kind of property gained the vote, and the way in which he voted.

The 1820 South Durham Poll book for the Stockton area provides some useful examples of poll book information. It mentions a George Nicholson of Egglescliffe, who lived in his own house worth forty shillings a year, and a William Pollock of Newcastle, who could vote because he owned property at Wolviston near Stockton.

There were three candidates at this election. Voters such as miller Robert Moon from Cornforth plumped for a single candidate. George Lodge of Stockton, who owned a house at Stockton tenanted by Ann Dunn, split his vote between two candidates.

As the nineteenth century progressed, the property qualification for voting was widened both in county and in borough. Gradually the accent moved away from property to the individual – at first adult males, then older adult females and, ultimately, nearly all adults over twenty-one (more recently eighteen) gained the franchise. As a result, the electoral registers for the middle to late-twentieth century tend to be fuller and more helpful to the family historian.

Finding More

Most of the major regional centres keep indexes to the Births, Deaths and Marriages records, and national websites abound, allowing fairly easy access to certificate details; the certificates still have to be paid for through official sources.

The censuses too gain much local coverage and can be viewed, usually on microfilm or microfiche, and are frequently supported by well-organised and helpful indexes. Yet again, national websites afford easy access to most census material.

Much electoral material lies scattered about the region and is covered fairly thoroughly below.

In Cumbria, census returns are arranged by historic county; those for Cumberland from 1841 to 1901 can be seen at Carlisle and Whitehaven. South Cumberland and Lancashire North of the Sands have returns at Barrow and Whitehaven, while those for Westmorland from 1841 to 1901 are available at the Whitehaven and Kendal Record offices.

The Northumberland Archives at Woodhorn provides a selection of useful material, including a list of freeholders from Hexham qualified to vote in 1701, and a number of election poll books for the county from the eighteenth century onwards. There are also lists of electors to be canvassed in North Northumberland during the election of 1832.

The Berwick office of the Northumberland Archives has copies of the census for North Northumberland from 1841 to 1891, and for the whole of Northumberland for 1901; some of the Berwick censuses have been transcribed and others are also indexed. This office also has electoral registers for Berwick,

Tweedmouth and Spittal available from 1835, with some gaps, and for other areas on microfilm from 1885 onwards.

The Blyth Local Studies Library holds copies of censuses for Northumberland from 1841 to 1901, while Hexham has electoral registers for the Southern Division of Northumberland from 1832 to 1900 and some beyond. It also holds Northumberland census returns from 1841 to 1901.

Morpeth Library has all the census material for Northumberland on film, fiche or CD although much material has now been transferred to Woodhorn.

Still in relation to Northumberland, the Tyne and Wear Archives has electoral and burgess records for some fifteen areas of Northumberland as well as nineteenth-century poll books for Hexham and Allendale. In relation to Tyneside, the same archives keeps electoral rolls and poll books, land tax and burgess lists including land tax returns for the Gosforth area of Newcastle from 1833 to 1946.

For South Shields there are also poll books, electoral registers and burgess lists from the nineteenth century.

Newcastle upon Tyne Central Library has the 1841 to 1901 census returns for Newcastle upon Tyne, and electoral registers for Newcastle from 1832 to date.

Gateshead Local Studies Centre keeps census records and electoral lists. At North Shields there are census returns for the area from 1841 to 1901, and an index to births, deaths and marriages.

South Shields Local Studies Centre has the census returns for the area from 1841 to 1901. The Berwick branch of the Northumberland Archives also keeps census returns for Newcastle and South Shields for 1901.

In relation to Wearside, electoral registers and some poll books from 1830 onwards are out on the open shelves at Sunderland Local Studies Library. Census material has been indexed by street and, in some cases, personal name.

For Modern County Durham, the Tyne and Wear Archives has a number of census returns on microfilm and microfiche.

The Durham County Library Collection in the Durham Record Office houses a host of electoral material covering a number of centuries and both city and county elections. There is also a thorough online guide to the extensive census material available on microfilm at the office.

Electoral registers exist for Darlington for the late-nineteenth century onwards, as well as a number of early poll books for the South Durham constituency. These can be found at Darlington Local Studies Centre.

Stockton Local Studies Library has census returns for the Stockton-on-Tees authority from 1841 onwards, and there is an unpublished index to the 1851 local census. The electoral registers here are mostly for the twentieth century although there is a poll book for Stockton's first personal election, the last one using poll books, in 1868.

Hartlepool Local Studies Library also has material relating to elections, electors and the national census, and further information can be gleaned by accessing its efficient Port Cities website.

Chapter Nine

LOCAL GOVERNMENT

This is a wide topic embracing a number of related areas, including the operation of local government itself, the treatment of poverty, law and order, health and burial. The common bond here, certainly up to the nineteenth century, was the parish and parish officers as they went about their business wearing their 'non-religious' hats. As a twentieth-century songwriter noted, in years past the parish and its church were central to the entire community:

> *The parish was a powerful place and the vestry not a room*
> *But the name for those who governed for the weaver at his loom*
> *Then the husbandman who tilled the soil would often form his views*
> *Round what he heard within these walls as he heard the weekly news*
> (Keith Gregson, *Limestone Walls*)

In some towns, especially market-towns, boroughs and corporations had been in existence since medieval times, and had powers to govern, establish laws and keep records. Before the industrial revolution, the North Country, like other parts of England, resembled a massive patchwork when it came to local government organisation and practice. Fortunately, this patchwork has left many records of use to the family historian, especially after the 1830s and 1840s, when Acts of Parliament clarified and extended the role of local government.

Governing the North Country

As with the parish registers recording baptism, marriage and burial, the survival of parish material relating to local government is often a case of luck. Where they do exist, researchers are likely to find references to the maintenance of highways, the workings of charity and apprenticeship and, in particular, the activities of the overseers charged with maintaining the poor. In some cases, the poor-law information may be recorded separately; in others it is simply mixed in with other information.

In the records of Stranton parish (later to embrace West Hartlepool), references appear to one pauper, Widdy Simpson, who was paid ten shillings by the overseers at Christmas in 1699. A year later, the same overseers paid the house rent of one Jean Hall. This information appears alongside details of the charges made for ringing the bells to celebrate a royal coronation and a victory in battle! The same records also mention the ratepayers who contributed towards the money distributed.

An interesting set of parish records for Rothbury in Northumberland has also survived. These include details of schoolhouse repairs, recipients of a local charity, and information on parishioners involved in both militia work and apprenticeship. Rothbury also maintained good overseers' records and, in general, such records may be of use to family historians. Their heyday finished in the 1830s when there was a substantial change in the way the poor were looked after under the official poor laws.

From the 1830s, parishes were gathered together into unions, usually centred on an industrial or market-town. Ratepayers in these unions elected boards of guardians. The guardians, in turn, had to see that the union had a suitable workhouse and that paupers received help or relief either in the workhouse or at home. Most of the unions set up in the 1830s survived without change in structure for almost a hundred years. One exception was the Stockton Poor Law Union, which had to be divided twice because of the growth of population. Out of the divisions came poor-law unions based on Hartlepool and Middlesbrough.

Records of ancestors may be found in workhouses or in their own homes 'on outdoor relief'. They can be discovered by reference to the census (the first informative census, in 1841, was taken soon after the first union workhouses were opened). The union records, many of which have survived in local and national archives, may refer to workhouse inmates. They are usually quite thorough on the elected guardians and professional staff, so you may be lucky if one of these happens to appear in your family tree.

In times of mass unemployment, the boards of guardians often opened stoneyards to occupy those out of work, and lists containing the names of those thus relieved are known to have survived.

Poor-law records can also be the starting point for examining hospital records, as many general hospitals started life as workhouses and gradually changed function in the twentieth century. There are many classic examples of such hospitals in the North Country, including those in Carlisle, Newcastle, Sunderland and Stockton. A few of the old workhouse buildings are still standing.

There were also 'private' and charitable hospitals, which kept their own records – the Cumberland Infirmary in Carlisle and the Royal Victoria Infirmary in Newcastle stand as good examples here.

Patients of what were then regarded as mental institutions often had their names and details recorded in both private institutions and workhouses. A list from the 1890s for the Northumberland County Asylum (later St George's, Morpeth) lists watermen, cabinetmakers, booksellers and miners, and gives details of age, address, religion and date of admission.

For centuries, the parish was also responsible for the maintenance of basic law and order through the constable. Under certain circumstances, he could also call on the assistance of special constables, as was the case in some Durham parishes. The wider development of policing is forever associated with the work of Robert Peel in the 1820s. In the North Country, the 1830s and 1840s proved significant decades in the formation of police forces. After the Municipal Corporations Act of 1835, forces were formed in Durham City and Historic County Durham. Gateshead, Durham and Sunderland also built up police forces in the 1830s, and Hartlepool developed a borough police force in 1851. From the 1840s, Durham County Constabulary had a chief constable and gained an important role in regional control. Important changes in the organisation of regional police forces came in the second part of the twentieth century. Police records can often be quite full and useful, especially if a North Country ancestor was in one of the forces.

Records have also survived relating to those at the other end of the legal spectrum, with court and prison records turning up in a number of North Country archives.

A good example of material available on law and order comes from papers handed over to the Tyne and Wear Archives in the 1990s. These contain details of prisoners in Newcastle Gaol in the 1870s and provide much useful information. Historian Barry Redfern has covered many of these prisoners in a book published in 2006.

Among the cases in these papers is that of eleven-year-old Ellen Woodman from Durham, who was given seven days hard labour for stealing scrap metal, and a twelve-year-old Castle Eden choirboy, Henry Stephenson, sentenced to two months for theft. Sixteen-year-old Michael Dixon, apprentice blacksmith at Armstrong's factory on the Tyne, received a fortnight in prison for being off work without permission.

Moving on to the more complex matter of municipal government, many towns and cities had rights and records dating back to medieval times. 'Old' Hartlepool, for example, was granted the same rights and freedoms as Newcastle during the reign of King John and had these extended and amended in the sixteenth and nineteenth centuries.

Carlisle was given its first Royal Charter in 1158. This and other charters gave rights to the collection of tolls and dues, and led to the rise in power of guilds and craftsmen. The records of such guilds and apprentices have often survived, as did those of mayors and corporations where they existed. In 1835, an Act of Parliament was passed to make local government more democratic and less dominated by small groups of individuals.

Local town and borough information can also be found relating to the un-reformed corporations. Sunderland, for example, has material relating to both freemen of the town (as it was then) and its ancient stallingers, or stallholders.

Improved local government organisation in the early-Victorian period paved the way for better burial arrangements and the introduction of public cemeteries. Many of these came after a Burial Act gave new powers to local authorities in the 1850s. In Sunderland, this led to the opening of a number of council cemeteries, including one at Mere Knolls to the north of the Wear and another at Bishopwearmouth to the south. Mere Knolls contains the grave of George William Atkinson, killed by empty coal tubs at the age of fourteen in 1904, as well as that of Robert Thompson, a well-known shipbuilder, who died in 1951. Bishopwearmouth contains the remains of local religious leader Canon Cockin, who was buried in 1889, and the tomb of Lewis Bittlestone of the 7th Battalion Durham Light Infantry (DLI), who died of wounds in October 1918.

A word here on the link between parishes and boroughs. In many northern towns in the nineteenth century, the little parish had to cope with all local government – a task often beyond it. West Hartlepool Improvement Commission eventually replaced Stranton parish but West Hartlepool itself did not become a borough until late in the nineteenth century. This was a difficult time for the amateurs concerned.

Barrow-in-Furness was the responsibility of the tiny parish of Dalton as the shipbuilding and metal producing town grew into an industrial giant and, like West Hartlepool, did not govern itself until it became quite a mature urban development. Information like this can be useful to the family historian when seeking out relevant resources.

Finding More

Local government, as ever, produced a mass of written material and much of it has survived in local archives and local studies centres. What is given here is little more than a representative sample of the type of evidence that can be found.

In Cumbria, the Carlisle office has numerous records relating to the Carlisle Poor Law Union as well as one or two from the Longtown Union and much relating to Dalston parish. There is also extensive information on infectious and isolation hospitals, and records from the former Cumberland and Westmorland Constabulary dating back to the early-nineteenth century.

The Kendal office has some records for the Westmorland County Hospital; at Barrow there are papers from the High Carley fever hospital and sanatorium plus others connected to healthcare in Barrow and Ulverston. There is some limited material on poor-law arrangements in Barrow and Ulverston.

The Whitehaven office has extensive material on the Cockermouth Poor Law Union.

The Tyne and Wear Archives also keeps transcripts and indexes for criminal records in Cumberland and Westmorland around the time of the Napoleonic Wars.

The Northumberland Archives at Woodhorn has material relating to the majority of post-1834 poor-law unions in the county. These include Alnwick, Bellingham, Castle Ward, Haltwhistle, Hexham, Morpeth and Rothbury.

Parish records, like those for Rothbury mentioned above, are well indexed. Woodhorn also has the records for the former Northumberland County Asylum, mentioned in the text above, and for Alnwick Infirmary, including some obituaries, matron's report books and many references to activities during both the world wars.

Here too are some Northumbrian burial-board records (for Haltwhistle and Embleton, for example). These are mostly twentieth-century, but those for the Ovingham Board go back into the nineteenth century.

The Berwick office has records relating to burial registers for civic cemeteries at Berwick, Tweedmouth and north Sunderland and a computer database for burials at Berwick from 1856 to 1888. Also here are poor-law records for the Northumberland unions based on Berwick itself, Belford and Glendale.

Hexham Local Studies Library has an indexed listing of burials of Hexham cemetery from 1859 to 1903, and the Tyne and Wear Archives keeps accounts of murders, trials and executions relating to Northumberland, as well as criminal registers and some twentieth-century records from the Northumberland Constabulary.

Other Northumberland records, concerning hospital and nursing associations, can also be accessed at the Tyne and Wear Archives. Here too, cemetery records exist for all areas of Tyneside, including the fascinating Ballast Hills in Newcastle, whose records date back into the late-eighteenth century. There are also hospital registers including those for Newcastle Lying-In Hospital, the Keelman's Hospital and Wallsend Infectious Diseases Hospital. The last records relate to admissions in the early-twentieth century.

Guild records and freemen records for Newcastle and Gateshead can be viewed here too, along with poor-law material, both parish and union. St Andrew's, Lamesley, in Gateshead, for example, has deposited bastardy bonds and pauper payments for the pre-union years, and Tynemouth Union has registers for paupers from the late-nineteenth century.

Newcastle has extensive rates records here, and there are nineteenth-century poor rates returns from North Shields in the early-nineteenth century. Good rates records exist for Whickham back into the eighteenth century.

Tyneside Crown Court material at the Tyne and Wear Archives relates mainly to the twentieth century. There are nineteenth-century quarter sessions records for Newcastle, and for Gateshead and South Shields County Court into nineteenth century.

Police records covering Gateshead go back to the 1830s and there are extensive records here too for Newcastle, South Shields and Tynemouth.

The County Record Office at Durham also has evidence from a number of local councils and from quarter sessions relating to Tyneside.

The records of Wearside cemeteries dating back to the 1850s can be found at the Tyne and Wear Archives, as can hospital records, including those for Houghton-le-Spring and Hetton Smallpox Hospital from the early-nineteenth century.

Also here are records for the former Sunderland mental hospital from a later date and other Sunderland hospitals, including the Eye Infirmary.

There are extensive Wearside poor-law records here too. These survive at parish and township level both before and after the Poor Law Amendment Act of 1834, and there are also records from the unions formed in the 1830s and some rate books for Sunderland and Bishopwearmouth.

Here too can be found records affecting the borough police force, formed in 1836.

The Sunderland Local Studies Library has various papers relating to the operation of local government.

Durham Record Office has the records of Durham County Council and other local councils in the County.

Darlington Local Studies Centre has local government burial records and miscellaneous poor-law records for Darlington and Haughton-Le-Skerne.

ERECTED
IN MEMORY OF
JOHN DIXON
WHO DEPARTED THIS LIFE
OCTOBER 11TH 1852
AGED 32 YEARS
HE WAS FOLLOWED TO THE
GRAVE BY A LARGE NUMBER OF
FRIENDS AND INHABITANTS

A reminder of the devastation caused by nineteenth-century disease.

At Stockton, there are also some early- and mid-nineteenth-century rate books available on microfilm.

The Tyne and Wear Archives has a list of licensed premises in Middlesbrough and Stockton with poor rate assessment and excise license duty for 1909–10.

Flesh on the Bones

This is not the most attractive topic for heritage and museum displays. There are, however, some small displays on the history and workings of local government in some of the larger museums. There may also be testimonies to the poor law where, despite massive rebuilding, some of the old workhouse buildings remain and, occasionally, old workhouse records still lie in the general hospitals.

The Guildhall Museum in the heart of Carlisle is worth a visit for those interested in guilds and their role in the running of local government. The Newcastle Story at Newcastle's Discovery Museum is also useful here.

Chapter Ten

MILITARY AND WARFARE

Although many areas of England can argue that they have had a 'difficult past', few are able to rival the North Country. For centuries, conflict was an everyday occurrence – battlefields criss-crossed the region's terrain – and Cumbria lays claim to the last important clashes on English soil, both domestic and international (one at Clifton Moor near Penrith and the other out on Solway Moss near the border).

From medieval to Tudor times, the Bishop of Durham was as much a warrior bishop as a prince bishop, and the sixteenth and seventeenth centuries saw family ties across the border territory as binding as any national loyalty.

Religion also played its part in both Tudor and Cromwellian times, and in the waning days of the Stuarts, when the Fifteen and the Forty-five drew on combatants from both sides of the border.

Little wonder that, as warfare became more organised and national records of warriors came to be kept, men (and later, women too) from the region should be at the forefront of activity.

The Army

Although the odd researcher may be able to trace military ancestry back to the Civil Wars or the Jacobite Rebellions, for most, the starting point has to be the organised armed forces, which developed from the eighteenth century onwards. Of these, three in particular dominated the region – regiments most commonly referred to as the Northumberland Fusiliers, The Durham Light Infantry and the Border Regiment.

The Northumberland Fusiliers has a long and distinguished history, stretching back into the seventeenth century and linking across to Ireland. Its main predecessor in the eighteenth century was the 5th Regiment of Foot. With the word 'Northumberland' added during this period, the much-heralded concept of Northumberland's 'Fighting Fifth' came into being. In the early days the regiment saw action in the Peninsula, Afghanistan and India.

First World War — Northumberland's Fighting Fifth.

In the nineteenth century the fusilier element was added, and the sweeping military reforms of the 1880s placed many Northumberland volunteer organisations alongside the local fusiliers in a single regiment. During the First World War, the regiment provided fifty-two battalions and a number carried the names of the Tyneside Scottish and Tyneside Irish.

These latter battalions suffered considerably on the Somme; the body of one of their number, George Nugent, was recently discovered near where he fell during the first wave of attacks. He was reburied with full military honours. The Fusiliers were present at most of the major battles of that war and the next conflict (there was a presence at Tobruk, El Alamein and Salerno, for example). After the Second World War, the regiment saw action in Korea, and in 1968 united with other fusiliers to form the Royal Regiment of Fusiliers.

The official history of the Durham Light Infantry begins in 1881 and finishes in 1968. In 1881, the regiment was organised as the county regiment of Durham, encompassing its Militia and Volunteer infantry and uniting two regular battalions: 1st Battalion, the 68th (Durham) Regiment of Foot (Light Infantry) and the 2nd Battalion, a redesignation of the 106th Regiment of Foot (Bombay Light Infantry).

The Durham part of this (the 68th) had been raised by a member of the Lambton family in the middle of the eighteenth century and had successfully served in the Peninsular and Crimean wars, where VCs were gained.

From the early-nineteenth century the regiment was made up of light infantry, who were often at the front in campaigns. Nowhere is this more apparent than in the First World War, where the Durhams were involved on virtually every front. By 1918, the regiment had raised forty-three battalions (including the 'Durham Pals'), twenty-two of which saw active service overseas and suffered a loss of life estimated at some thirteen thousand.

There was a similar heavy involvement in the Second World War, where a DLI man, Richard Annand of the 2nd Battalion, DLI, became the very first soldier to gain a Victoria Cross in the conflict.

The post-war period brought service in major areas, including Korea and Borneo, before a merger with others into the wider Light Infantry in the 1960s.

The army reforms of the late-nineteenth century also saw the formation of the Border Regiment from the Cumberland and Westmorland Regiments, the local militias and the Cumberland and Westmorland Volunteers.

The history of the Border Regiment (later known as the King's Own Border Regiment) stretches back to the eighteenth century and Lord Lucas's Regiment. The regiment has long been associated with many of the areas

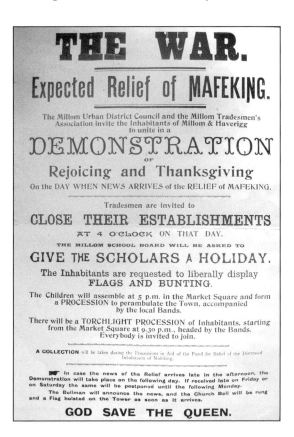

Millom learns of the Relief of Mafeking, Boer War.

making up modern Cumbria, and its connection with Carlisle Castle started at a fairly early date.

During the nineteenth century, the 34th (Cumberland) Regiment and the 55th (Westmorland) Regiment were involved in the Napoleonic and Crimean Wars, where VCs were won. One battalion plus some of the volunteers served in South Africa during the Boer War.

Like the other regional regiments, the Border Regiment was heavily involved in both major conflicts of the twentieth century, including service at Gallipolli and in the trenches in the First World War, and in Holland and Burma during the Second World War.

The regiment's long links with the castle came to an end in 1959 when it amalgamated with the King's Own and became the King's Own Border Regiment.

Northern ancestors may also be discovered in other armed organisations, such as the militia, yeomanry or mid-nineteenth century volunteers (often scorned in North-Eastern music hall songs).

The Northumberland and Newcastle Volunteer Cavalry, for example, was raised in 1819. In 1876 it became the Northumberland Hussars. Yeomanry and Imperial Yeomanry Companies served in the Boer War.

Originally formed to help in cases of civil disturbance, the hussars saw action in both world wars in mobile vehicles. In 1947 they were affiliated to

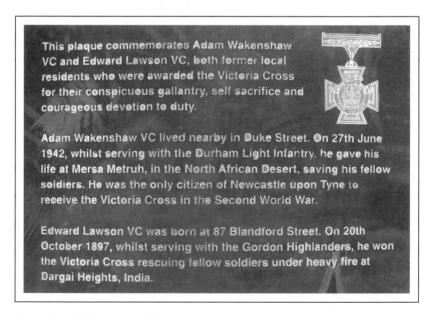

This plaque commemorates Adam Wakenshaw VC and Edward Lawson VC, both former local residents who were awarded the Victoria Cross for their conspicuous gallantry, self sacrifice and courageous devotion to duty.

Adam Wakenshaw VC lived nearby in Duke Street. On 27th June 1942, whilst serving with the Durham Light Infantry, he gave his life at Mersa Metruh, in the North African Desert, saving his fellow soldiers. He was the only citizen of Newcastle upon Tyne to receive the Victoria Cross in the Second World War.

Edward Lawson VC was born at 87 Blandford Street. On 20th October 1897, whilst serving with the Gordon Highlanders, he won the Victoria Cross rescuing fellow soldiers under heavy fire at Dargai Heights, India.

North-East VC heroes recalled in Newcastle.

Millom's Stephens brothers survive the First World War.

the 15/19 The King's Royal Hussars and, in 1971, moved with others into the Queen's Own Yeomanry.

There were other regiments with toeholds in the area, notably the Green Howards, centred for years on Richmond and drawing from North Yorkshire, and The King's Own Scottish Borderers, with strong Berwick connections.

Lancashire regiments drew in men from Barrow-in-Furness and its areas of influence southwards towards Preston.

Despite the local links of many of these regiments, they were not always packed with local men. A valuable published list of the Hartlepools' dead from the First World War shows that they were serving in regiments far and wide.

Three Stephens brothers, for example, all born in Millom, Cumbria, in the 1880s, ended up in the Royal Engineers, Royal Artillery and King's Liverpool Rifles during the First World War.

The Navy

If the army attracted many men from the North Country, it was equally natural that others from the region, and from the coastal areas in particular, should serve in the Royal Navy. Apart from shipbuilding and the maritime trade, ports up and down the coasts, such as Hartlepool, Newcastle and Berwick had played important roles in provisioning the navy in time of war with the Scots. Barrow-in-Furness and Tyneside also produced warships and it was natural that local lads often wanted to serve in local ships.

Equally, work done for the bicentenary of the Battle of Trafalgar in 1805 revealed the important connection between the North-East, in particular, and the Royal Navy in Napoleonic times. When volunteers were not enough to fill the navy, an open coastline with few places to hide made the unwilling easy meat for the press gangs, and stories abound of Tyneside and Wearside men taken by the gang, from up in the collieries as well as along the coast. As a

Memorial to Jack Crawford, naval hero, Sunderland.

result, many traditional press-gang songs also have their origins in the North-East.

The region also produced a number of famous sailors, not least Jack Crawford, 'the hero of Camperdown' (from Sunderland), and Admiral Collingwood from Morpeth, who commanded the fleet at Trafalgar after the death of Nelson.

Fletcher Christian, famous for his involvement with the mutiny on the *Bounty*, was born near Cockermouth and had a North-Eastern compatriot on the *Bounty* itself in the shape of one Thomas McIntosh. The American naval raider John Paul Jones also had family links with the Solway.

Master mariner John Charles Pottinger, from South Shields, was decorated in the First World War for saving his cargo after a submarine attack. His son, also a merchant captain, was prisoner on the *Graf Spee* during the Battle of the River Plate in 1939. Their cousin Betty Stephens, from Barrow-in-Furness, served as a telephone operator in the Fleet Air Arm in the 1940s.

Men from the North served on and protected the Atlantic convoys, and Lord Mountbatten famously commanded a vessel adopted by the people of Shields.

In the Air

From the First World War onwards, many would see service in the Royal Flying Corps, later the Royal Air Force. Harold Gregson, a tinsmith by trade, born in Barrow-in-Furness, first served in a Lancashire regiment early in the First World War, before moving into the Royal Flying Corps. He spent most of the war at Yate, near Bristol, where his skills would have been used in providing the metal elements of warplanes.

During the same war, there was a small airfield on one of Sunderland's town moors, as an aerodrome was developed at Hylton/Usworth between Sunderland and Washington. It was constructed initially to protect against zeppelin attacks, and zeppelins were brought down in the area. It was used by the Auxiliary Air Force in the inter-war years and by regular units towards the outbreak of the next war. The aerodrome was a target in wartime and there were dogfights nearby. Wearside fighter ace Joe Kayll, who was shot down and became a well-known escape officer, did much of his training here. The aerodrome's life ended in 1984 and it is part of the Nissan car plant today.

Aircraft were produced in Newcastle for the armed forces and there was an important base on the site of the modern Durham Tees Valley Airport.

During the Second World War, aerodromes in Cumbria too had a military purpose, such as the Royal Naval Air Service stations at Anthorn and Silloth. The Solway coast was also marked out for use in bombing practice (the marks are still in evidence).

Civilians at War

Documents in major centres around the region recall important ancestral links with the Home Front during the main twentieth-century conflicts. In the First World War, there were more civilian casualties than are often recognised. Both east and west coasts saw minor submarine raids as well as zeppelin raids.

Serious damage was caused to places such as Sunderland, and tales are told of zeppelins brought down and excitement in the sky around the Hartlepools. It was here that the worst civilian casualties of the war came, in December 1914, when both Hartlepool and West Hartlepool were attacked from the sea by German surface raiders. Approximately 150 people died as a result of the attack, and there were hundreds wounded and massive damage done to both public and private property. The only target considered legitimate at the time was a gun emplacement at Hartlepool, where there were a number of military casualties. The enemy's aim was either woefully poor or simply indiscriminate, and the numbers of local men joining the armed forces increased soon after. Many of the dead are mentioned by name in books about the attack.

The Second World War also saw significant casualties and damage across the region. All the heavy industrial areas were targeted and considerable evacuation to the countryside took place (Newcastle Royal Grammar School, for example, was completely resettled in rural Cumbria).

Towns and cities with shipbuilding and repairing facilities were particularly vulnerable, with Newcastle, Sunderland and Barrow-in-Furness (to name but three), suffering as a result of air raids.

Before joining the Fleet Air Arm, Betty Gregson née Stephens was a telephonist in Barrow-in-Furness and recalls receiving messages from the Liverpool Exchange that Liverpool had been overflown by enemy aircraft; Barrow was usually the night's target and her next call was to the siren operator.

Railway stations in Barrow and Sunderland were extensively damaged and tales are told of the damage done on the night that one of the main food warehouses in Newcastle received a direct hit.

As one website notes, 'This war was fought by Air Raid Wardens, Land Girls, Munitions Workers, Bevan Boys, Home Guards, Auxiliary Firemen, plus mothers and children,' and there is every chance that evidence for their experiences will have survived.

Finding Out

When it comes to finding out about individual military ancestors, museums, and regimental museums in particular, can often be as useful in terms of resources as the more usual archives (see Flesh on the Bones below). Many records of soldiers, sailors and airmen are also likely to be found at national rather than local level, especially at The National Archives, and it is worth repeating that men did not always serve in local regiments. Nevertheless, there remains a great deal of useful material kept locally and it is worth exploring carefully for early militia material, which turns up on occasions.

The Cumbria Archive Services keeps a range of fascinating material related to this topic. At Whitehaven, there are Pennington family letters relating to active service during the Crimean War, and at the Barrow office the papers of Surveyor and Estate Agent Charles G Lowden contain extensive references to instances of Second World War damage.

The Carlisle Archives has material relating to the Transvaal War Fund during the Boer War, the letters of First World War pacifist Catherine Marshall from Keswick and documents on Home Front arrangements during both world wars.

The Northumberland Archives has recordings made in the 1970s concerning active service in the First World War and Second World War, and papers from

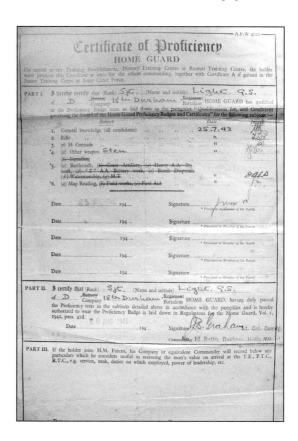

The Home Front in the Second World War – a West Hartlepool Home Guard certificate of proficiency.

the Thomas Knight Memorial Hospital at Blyth concerning war casualties (civilian and non-civilian).

At the Tyne and Wear Archives, there are Tyneside records from the First World War, including Civil Defence information, absent voters lists and details of medical and charitable care in Newcastle. Records for the Second World War include those on civilian casualties admitted to hospital in Whickham in 1941 and those for Whitley Bay from 1939 to 1941.

The Tyne and Wear Archives also has Wearside records for both major twentieth-century conflicts. Written guides point to material on recruitment, treatment of immigrants, war memorials and rolls of honour, as well as evidence dealing with life on the Home Front.

The Regimental Archive of the DLI has been transferred to the Durham County Record Office, where it is has been fully catalogued and made available to researchers. The archives lie conveniently close to the regimental museum (for details of the museum see below), but a visit to the well-organised website first is highly recommended. Here can be found details of the regimental records and the numerous photographs, which have been digitally recorded and catalogued.

In relation to Nelson's Navy, historian Tony Barrow produced a book about the North Country sailors at Trafalgar in time for the bicentenary of the battle. In this book, he noted that the North-East of England 'contained one of the most important concentrations of skilled mariners anywhere in the United Kingdom'. The combined ports of Newcastle and Sunderland came second after London in the numbers they were to provide for the navy under the quota acts.

Hundreds from the old counties of Northumberland and Durham fought at Trafalgar. Over twenty of them survived and were awarded the Trafalgar medal, which was not given out until over forty years after the battle. On the *Colossus* alone there were at least fifty men with North Country connections and in the battle itself, sixty were killed, wounded or died as a result of wounds. Barrow's book is an excellent resource for finding out about these men, who are often noted by name and place of origin.

Flesh on the Bones

The Castle Museum in Carlisle will be of great interest to anyone with ancestral involvement in the Jacobite Rebellion of 1745, which is featured in a number of displays.

The Border and King's Own Royal Border Regimental Museum, in Queen Mary's Tower in the castle, covers the history of the old county of Cumberland's county infantry regiment. Here there are two major rooms packed with medals, muster rolls and memorabilia, and plans are afoot to move and improve the displays and facilities. This museum should be the starting point for anyone with ancestors in the regiment.

There is also an Aviation Museum at Carlisle Airport for those with a family interest in wartime RAF Cumbria or the development of post-war rocketry. Spadeadam, just further west, was the site of important developments in space technology in the years after the Second World War.

Maryport on the Cumbrian coast has an interesting link with naval history. Perched above the Sea Brows, which overlook the Solway Firth from what is known as The Promenade, is the Royal Naval Reserve Station (the 'Battery'). Opened in 1886, it was home to up to two hundred reservists who were trained there annually; the building also houses the coastguard station.

In Berwick, the UK's first purpose-built barracks is home to a complex of museums dealing with the history of the area. The town walls, which date from Tudor times, are said to be the best-preserved in Europe and visitors can walk around them.

Those interested in their reiving past can find out what a defended pele tower was like by popping into Preston Tower at Chathill, just off the A1. Built in the fourteenth century and furnished in contemporary style, it is one of the few to have survived.

Links with the (Royal) Northumberland Fusiliers can be traced at the regimental museum, which has been situated in the Abbot's Tower at Alnwick Castle since 1970.

A great deal of work has gone into improving the maintenance of records in recent years and the museum now maintains a collection of uniforms, medals, weapons, paintings and memorabilia relating to the various historical campaigns in which the regiment has fought. This museum is also the repository of all archival information that relates to the former regiment and shows its continuation as part of the Royal Regiment of Fusiliers.

On Tyneside, the A Soldier's Life Gallery at the Discovery Museum covers the history of the regular 15/19 The King's Royal Hussars and the Territorial Northumberland Fusiliers from their North-Eastern origins onwards. The displays give a remarkable insight into the life of the cavalry soldier who later served in tanks. The Newcastle Story in the same museum currently displays some of the military equipment belonging to George Nugent, mentioned above.

At South Shields Museum, a small area of the gallery is dedicated to the region in wartime, with some displays linked to the novels of Catherine Cookson.

At Washington F Pit Museum there is a long list of the names of those from local collieries who served in the First World War.

Wearside also has a small but fascinating museum dedicated to aircraft history with many artefacts relating to the airfield at Usworth.

In Modern County Durham, The Durham Light Infantry Museum, set in delightful grounds close to the city centre, is a major centre. It covers the story of the regiment back into the eighteenth century with particular emphasis on the two world wars of the twentieth century. Themes covered include

Coins and Medals, Costume and Textiles, Land Transport, Personalities, Weapons and War. The displays look particularly at the experience of war, using letter and diary extracts featuring the actual voices of soldiers. There is also much of interest about life on the Home Front in the area during the Second World War.

One of the highlights of the museum is the collection of over three thousand medals awarded to over one thousand men who served in the regiment. The medals displayed were awarded to Durham Light Infantry soldiers who fought in the regiment, and date from the Peninsular War battles against Napoleon two hundred years ago to the last campaign in Borneo in the 1960s. Medals range from the highest gallantry award – the Victoria Cross – to local medals presented to DLI soldiers by the grateful people of communities in the county. All of the medals are on display in the DLI Museum's Medal Room.

The museum website also guides researchers to the sound clips made by the Imperial War Museum's Department of Sound. These include recordings of the voices of soldiers who fought with the Durham Light Infantry during the Second World War.

In County Durham there is a heritage site, which may be of interest to those tracing German and Italian ancestry. This forms the refurbished Harperley POW Camp Heritage site. Constructed late in the Second World War to house Italian and German prisoners, it is one of the most complete camps left. Much work has been done on the site in recent years, and key features are murals drawn by homesick prisoners and a purpose-built theatre.

The First World War bombardment of the Hartlepools is marked in modern Hartlepool in a number of ways. The site of the Heugh Battery, which lay at the centre of the raid, has been recently restored and there are displays and memorabilia in the Museum of Hartlepool.

The Historic Quay at Hartlepool is more a national than a regional centre but will be of interest to anyone with ancestors who were in Nelson's Navy. Here can be seen the refurbished *Trincomalee*, 'the last of Nelson's frigates'.

Both museums in Stockton – at Preston Hall and Green Dragon Yard – have displays connected to local weapons and warfare.

The website of the Dorman Museum at Middlesbrough contains testimonies on the Home Front in the Second World War and these have been kept online after a successful 'All Clear' exhibition shown in 2005/6.

Chapter Eleven

EDUCATION

Researchers seeking details of the education of North Country ancestors face problems similar to those encountered by researchers in other regions of England, namely the poverty of early educational record-keeping. Government organisation of education was in its infancy about the time that useful census material and civil registration came into being in the 1830s and 1840s and, even later in the century, much of the choice relating to making education compulsory and/or 'free' lay in local hands. Despite this, records improved during the school-board era (from 1870 until the end of the century), as 'going to school' gradually became a habit.

Before the introduction of compulsory education, and officers with the powers to enforce it, wealth, faith, family attitudes and, in some cases, good fortune influenced the decision whether a youngster was educated or not. Under such circumstances, it is hardly surprising to find the records for education rather haphazard, particularly before the final quarter of the nineteenth century.

North Country Education

In the days before government interest in education (usually noted as the 1830s at the earliest), the main schools in operation were dame schools, charity schools and Sunday schools, in addition to grammar schools and public schools for the wealthier section of society. This said, one of the region's most famous sons, Bede, enjoyed the fruits of a monastic education on the coast of Historic Durham many years before the Norman Conquest. Though of humble origins, he became a true academic and seized an opportunity available to few in the centuries that were to follow.

Some schools emerged from among the religious establishments of medieval times, for example, the former Carlisle Grammar School (now Trinity School). Tradition has it that Cuthbert founded the school in the seventh century. It was certainly functioning as a monastery school in the twelfth century and became the grammar school of the cathedral during the reign of Henry VIII.

The origins of the Royal Grammar School at Newcastle are somewhat different. Its roots go back to the sixteenth century and it was funded by a private individual. With some exceptions, the school provided for the education of the wealthier. From RGS emerged John Lilburne, the seventeenth-century leveller; Lord Eldon, Chancellor of England in the early-nineteenth century, and Cuthbert Collingwood, who took control of the British fleet at Trafalgar after the death of Nelson.

The region also has its share of public schools, such as St Bees and Sedbergh in the west and Durham School and Barnard Castle in the east. Often noted for their sporting prowess, such schools provided for boarders from outside the area as much as for local pupils.

Private education was not always up to scratch and it is interesting to note that Dickens gained the evidence for the creation of his infamous Dotheboys Hall from an establishment near Barnard Castle.

Dame schools were usually found in private homes and regarded as little more than baby-sitting services; they have left few records although local histories sometimes refer to their existence. Here and in charity schools, people brought up in poverty could still gain some form of education. As Ivy Pinchbeck noted of rural education in the early-nineteenth century, 'While leaving much to be desired' it was 'not altogether lacking.'

A classic example of this is the education of the Cumberland Bard, Robert Anderson, who has left a lovely account of his own school experience in the 1770s:

> At an early age, I was placed in a Charity School . . . Blessed be the Institutors and encouragers of such seminaries; who place the offspring of the labouring classes in the true road to knowledge and happiness in a future state. Still do I remember the neat dress, slow speech, placid countenance, nay every feature of good old Mrs Addison, the teacher . . . she only gave instruction in reading and plain sewing.

Later in his memoir, Anderson recalls a male teacher, 'a long, lean, needy pretender to knowledge' who inspired a love of nature and poetry in his young charge as the pair ploughed their way through *Reading Made Easy* and Dyche's *Spelling Book*.

In the North-East, the story of George and Robert Stephenson makes interesting reading. George, the great engineer much adored by self-helper Samuel Smiles, taught himself to read when aged eighteen. In consequence, he sent his son Robert to the local village school at Longbenton and, about the time of the battle of Waterloo, to Bruce's Academy in Newcastle. George also insisted that his son spent time in the library of the Literary and Philosophical Society. Robert, too, became a great engineer, claiming the construction of the High Level Bridge across the Tyne as one of his major successes.

In this context, too, the small north Cumbrian village of Burgh-by-Sands can be seen as a good example. It had 'three small schools, but not endowed' in the early-nineteenth century. One of them was founded on the generosity of Richard Hodgson who 'left 100 l [£100]: to which is added 12s 2d, issuing out of some lands, and the interest of 12 l stock, which is applied to the repairs of the school-house'.

The eighteenth-century Cumbrian writer Susanna Blamire wrote about her local village school in an epic poem called *Stoklewath*. The description is remarkably clear and the school surprisingly recognisable. Some pupils rush home for dinner while others have a packed lunch. They taunt the crabby old schoolmistress who has kept a naughty pupil in over the dinner hour and they play the kind of games still pursued in modern schoolyards, including football or 'foot-ball':

> *For races some, but more for foot-ball cry*
> *Mark out their ground and toss the ball on high*

Although of the manorial class, Susanna Blamire actually attended the local primary school she mentions in her poem. An aunt who was an avid reader then took over her education, encouraging the youngster to read too. The poetess was lucky here; as a biographer notes, there were no 'boarding schools in those days for the education of young ladies – at least in those parts'.

Slightly later, in the early-nineteenth century, Cumbrian writer Thomas Sanderson provides a delightful description of a typical local schoolmaster:

Few occupations are attended with more labour and less profit than that of a country schoolmaster. In Cumberland his income seldom exceeds thirty pounds a year for which he teaches forty or fifty scholars during nine or ten hours of the day.

A couple of reports from the middle of the nineteenth century suggest that in Northumberland there were more schools and education for rural children than in most places in the country – also that parents made every effort to get their children some schooling.

Susanna Blamire wrote a charming description of a village school.

A village primary school – Burgh-by-Sands, Cumbria.

Elsewhere, the news was not so good. Nearly all reports in the nineteenth century tell of a complete lack of educational facilities for girls in the colliery villages. Writers particularly mentioned this as they noted the importance of females in the community; they had a great influence on family life and were often left, though uneducated themselves, to educate the children. The same writers also drew the conclusion that Sunday schools were not a great success in these areas.

There are, of course, exceptions to the rules. In Sunderland many poor girls benefited from an education at the Donnison School, which was set up after a £1,500 bequest in 1778. The school was still going strong in the nineteenth century and oral histories collected recently put all connected with the establishment in a favourable light.

As far as boys were concerned, a government inspector wrote in the early-1840s of the average Durham pit lad:

> Previous to going down the pit, his education, when he had any, generally consisted of a little reading got from the village-school-mistress. After he went to work, little time for education could be spared, unless for want of demand, the pits were not at full work.

When Alexander Ball, an eighteen-year-old miner at Monkwearmouth Colliery, was asked about his childhood education about the same time, the interviewer was able to note:

> Can read an easy book. Writes very little; writes his name. Does not go to night-school, but sometimes goes to Sunday-school.

By the middle of the nineteenth century, more elementary education was available as a result of the battle between the Church of England and nonconformist churches, and many a village school owes its foundation to this conflict.

In 1870, Gladstone's government put education at the top of its list and passed an act enabling local authorities to tackle the shortage of schools where it was deemed necessary. The act was a little complicated but it allowed local authorities to raise local taxes to build Board schools where they were needed. Many still alive today will be familiar with the old school-board buildings, which are still functional in some older schools.

Between 1870 and 1902, school boards were set up all over the region; by the turn of the century, most youngsters were at school and a system of attendance-checking was in operation. Tommy Armstrong, a Durham pitman, wrote a memorable song about his own youthful clashes with the School Bobby, or school-board man, the chorus of which runs:

> *Send your bairns to school*
> *Learn them all you can*
> *Make scholarship your faithful friend*
> *And you'll never see the School Board Man.*

Local Education Authorities replaced school boards soon after the death of Queen Victoria, and the twentieth century saw a move towards secondary education. By the 1930s, grammar schools were taking in pupils from different social groups, although many still completed their education by early teenage. By the 1970s, the move to comprehesive education had been made and the school leaving age had been raised to sixteen.

Over the years, the region has also seen changes in provision for further education. In Sunderland, for example, the technical college eventually merged into the polytechnic system of the 1960s, then into the wider university system. There have been similar developments in Cumbria, with educational facilities in both Carlisle and Ambleside tied into a university college in North Lancashire. Teesside too has its own popular university, based in the very heart of Middlesbrough.

In terms of the older universities, Durham University is one of the oldest and most treasured in the country. One of its former colleges, King's Newcastle, known for its medical training in the past, broke off to form a separate university in Newcastle in the 1960s. Both have produced famous graduates in many fields. More interestingly, perhaps, they brought many people (including my wife and me) into the North-East to settle on a permanent basis.

Finding More

Most of the major regional archives have extensive records relating to education; these can usually be checked by visiting the relevant websites.

Records often include plans and building details, logbooks, minutes, punishment books and photographs. The survival of admission and discharge registers, which are most likely to be of use to family historians, is, as in many education-related issues, a case of 'pot luck'. Where they do survive, these are mostly for the twentieth century.

The Cumbrian Archives are fairly well served with school material. The Carlisle office has extensive records relating to the now defunct Friends School at Wigton, as well as good evidence for education in Dalston, just outside Carlisle, and many references to village and parish education.

The Barrow office has interesting education material, including the nineteenth-century admission registers for the Sunday school at St Anne's, Thwaites, and a nineteenth-century list of book-borrowers for the Sunday school at St Mary's, Ulverston.

The Kendal office has a great deal of school information originating in the Westmorland and Kendal Councils, and interesting material on education concerning the Society of Friends, not all of it local.

The Northumberland County Archives stores much material related to education, including some late-nineteenth-century admissions for Lowick County Primary School and the records of Ulgham Church School.

The education material at the Tyne and Wear Archives is well organised and indexed with separate guides for schools and related material in North Tyneside, South Tyneside, Wearside, Newcastle and Gateshead.

As in most cases, logbooks and minutes are more common than attendance registers although there are some early-twentieth-century registers for Gateshead and some for Sunderland's Bede School, both boys and girls, stretching back into the nineteenth century.

Documents relating to schools in Modern and Historic County Durham can be accessed through the Durham County Record Office website. This office has records such as admissions registers for Trimdon Colliery Boys School during the nineteenth century and Deaf Hill Council School, Girls' department from the early part of the twentieth century.

The education references in the Teesside Archives include a number of schools and authorities but most of them relate to the more technical side of administration in Hartlepool and Middlesbrough in particular.

Some material may still remain with schools, as in the case of St Bees public school in Cumbria. Many of the older schools have also produced histories; in the twentieth century, for example, a couple of large books were published on the subject of the history of Newcastle Royal Grammar.

As do older sports clubs, these schools often display photographs of past pupils in their buildings, particularly when the pupils were part of successful sports teams.

Flesh on the Bones

Many of the museums and heritage sites put flesh on the bones of local education through small displays of photographs or actual reconstructed classrooms. Two good examples are at the North of England Open Air Museum at Beamish and the Captain Cook Schoolroom Museum at Great Ayton on the very southern fringe of the region.

At Beamish, the colliery village contains the Beamish Board School, which opened just up the road at East Stanley in the dying years of the nineteenth century. This school was able to house some 200 children in three classrooms. Lessons are often carried out here and celebrations of Sunday school education have also taken place on the site.

The Captain Cook Schoolroom Museum is housed in a building once used as a charity school, which was founded in 1704 by Michael Postgate, a local landowner. It was here, between 1736 and 1740, that Captain James Cook received his early education.

Chapter Twelve

DIALECT AND DIET

Dialect

Dialect (including accent) can be a delicate issue; at times it is almost easier to be a total outsider, recognising a speaker's origins as simply 'Cumbrian' or 'North-Eastern'. Once inside the region and in the know, you will find matters more complex, with any number of experts around willing to point out minor discrepancies.

Although time, the modern broadcast media and ease of travel have combined to wear away many features of dialect, enough evidence remains – written, recorded and spoken – to give some flavour of the older ancestral tongues. Cumbria, for example, hosted myriad different dialects and, in terms of using the simple word 'Cumbrian', the situation has not been helped by the fairly recent merging of Cumberland and Westmorland.

The dialects of the south of Cumbria contain elements of those of Lancashire, Yorkshire and County Durham. Those in the north contain elements of those of Scotland and Northumberland. The Lake District too can claim a dialect of its own, with its valleys and hills ensuring plenty of local variation. Writing in the middle of the nineteenth century, West Cumbrian poet and writer Alexander Craig Gibson claimed that his neighbours alone spoke the 'unadulterated Old-Norse-rooted Cumbrian vernacular'.

Here is not the place to go into detailed discussion on these issues. Best perhaps to look at some examples of the type of language Cumbrian ancestors might have used. Dialect does not often transfer well to the page; the aim of the dialect writer is simply to convey the sounds as they are heard, a practice that can in itself lead to controversy.

Gibson provides us with an example of his West Cumbrian dialect in a poem he wrote about an old fiddle player and dancing master called Ben Wells (or Wales). The following lines suggest that those who knew him would never forget the old musician:

Noo, poor Ben Wales is deid an' gean
His marrow willn't seun be seen;
But rare top dancers many a yan
He's left to keep his memory green

Noo for 'now' and *yan* for 'one' are typical of this accent and the word *marrow*, or *marra*, remains in common use across the region to mean many different things from a friend and a special workmate to somebody from West Cumberland.

Gibson also tried to reproduce the High Furness accent in a poem where a poor old man discusses life's lot with his wife. In this extract he suggests that all people are basically the same and fortune's wheel might still turn things round:

An' if we's pooer, we s'sham' nin
For rich fooak's no'but fooak
An wha' can tell, we's happen dra
Sum prize fray fortun's pooak

Dialect retains its popularity in certain areas.

Nin for 'none', *fooak* for 'folk' and *pooak*, or *poke*, for purse are all of interest here in a passage with strong Lancastrian influences.

A similar battle rages on the eastern side of the Pennines, where insiders can detect considerable differences in local dialect whereas outsiders often speak of a blanket 'Geordie' dialect and accent from Tweed to Tees. Without getting too involved, one can spot a handful of key dialects at the very least in this part of the region.

Northumbrians are particularly proud of their dialect, or language, as they prefer to call it, and are extremely proactive in preserving it. In some cases this includes the magnificent rolling 'r' still to be found in many parts of the county.

The Northumbrian dialect differs from that of Tyneside, which, in turn, differs from that found on Wearside. Sometimes it is something as simple as lilt; sometimes the pronunciation of single words such as 'make' (*myek* or *makk*) and 'take' (*tyek* and *takk*).

In the days when the coalmines were in operation, the folk living in the major urban parts of Historic County Durham knew if the owner came from 'the collieries' by his or her accent. For those living in the region too, the 'Geordie twang' (if there is such a thing) appears to fade out as Historic County Durham sweeps down onto the Tees Plain.

Most of those born and raised in the Tees Valley, certainly towards the east, tend to be identifiable by the flatter tones associated with Yorkshire. They may well describe their Teesside home as *Teesaard*.

In the North-East heartland, youngsters often chanted the following request for coins as a wedding party came out of church. *Ha'penny* for 'halfpenny' and *oot* for 'out' give some flavour of the North-Eastern accent. The *spoot*, or *spout*, is defined here as prison but the phrase surrounding it sometimes means simply that all possessions have been pawned.

> *Hi, canny man, ha' your ha'penny oot*
> *Me father's in the spoot and I canna get him oot*
> *Hi, canny man, ha' your ha'penny oot*

Some lines from a song written in the Tyneside dialect around 1800 afford another good example:

> *Bout Lunnon aw'd heerd sec wonderful spokes*
> *That the streets were a' cover'd wi' guineas:*
> *The hooses sae fine, and sec grandees the folks*
> *To them huz i' the North were but ninnies*

Wi for 'with' and *hooses* for 'houses' should be noted here.

As if to cement regional differences, it has not gone unnoticed that the West Cumbrian town of Workington, described locally as *Wukkinton*, is known as *War-kinton* on Tyneside and *Where-kinton* in the Hartlepool district.

Diet

As in dialect, there were variations in diet, certainly as far as those in the lower and middle areas of society were concerned. Although Tourist Cumbria makes great play today on its links to Cumberland sausage, ham and rum butter, earlier references paint a wider and more interesting picture. In 1811, the Cumbrian writer Jollie wrote of the food eaten in the rural part of Cumberland. The bread, he suggests, was either barley or barley and rye and generally leavened, although he states that unleavened bread known as *scons*, or *bannocks*, was more common in the border area.

Both breakfast and supper consisted of 'hasty pudding', a thick potage based on oatmeal and filled out to taste, with butter, milk or treacle. In rather pompous style, he notes that such food

> swelled the massy bulk and large limbs of thousands of rustics, and preserved them to a good age unattacked by the train of diseases attended in modern luxury having latterly been a little ousted by tea and butcher's meat.

The historic role of meat in the life of 'working people' makes for an interesting study; the indications are that some meats were not affordable, even to those who produced them. However, Jollie does note that, in the early-nineteenth century, farmers were starting to keep back a little more beef and mutton for their own use. At the same time, a piece of bacon went down well with its fat poured over a plate filled with mashed potato.

Crowdy, also known across the border, was also eaten; this consisted of oatmeal and beef or mutton marrow, and a *cow'd-lword* was made up of oatmeal, tallow, suet and hog's lard.

Writing around a decade later, another Cumbrian, Thomas Sanderson, provides a wonderful description of a North Cumbrian cheese known as *Whyllymer*, or *Rosley Cheshire*: 'as remarkable for its poverty as that of Stilton is for its richness'. So hard was it that it challenged the sharpest knife and gave unwanted exercise to the teeth.

Sanderson also makes frequent reference to ale, whisky, rum and tea. The whisky was taken with a little water and often drunk when the rum had run out (West Cumbrian links with the Caribbean ensured a good smuggling trade here).

The region as a whole abounds with amusing tales concerning the introduction of tea into everyday life in the late-eighteenth century. Some of the older generation apparently did not know what to do with it and added salt to the leaves to make into a broth. This was found to be rather bitter!

In the North-East, the song 'Billy Boy', written down by a Northumberland-born song collector, names some of the delicacies around in the late-eighteenth century. These include the *gairdle cake* and *singin' hinnies*. In a note, the collector points out that *gairdle cakes* (there are different spellings) were cakes baked on a griddle; *singin' hinnies* were a species of Sally Lunn teacake, only larger. They were usually plentifully besprinkled with currants, in which case they were 'designated by pitmen as *singin hinnies with smaa co fizzors* (small coal fizzers)'.

'Billy Boy' also mentions Irish Stew, which is hardly surprising considering the number of immigrants from the Emerald Isle.

Towns and larger villages often had a cook shop or meat house where meat was taken to be cooked if the home had no large oven of its own.

Tommy Armstrong, the pitman poet, wrote a wonderful ditty about a group of colliery lads who used to steal pies as they cooled on the meat-house windowsill. The owner cooked them a special *Hedgehog Pie*. They ate it and became the laughing stock of the community as they broke out in prickles, or *proggles*.

As regards drink, the twentieth century saw the introduction of the world-famous Newcastle Brown Ale, a 'rich coloured brew with a strength and flavour of its own'. *Broon*, or *The Dog*, as it is still known, started up in the 1920s with its strange canine nickname apparently linked to the family pet, which was always 'taken for a walk' in the evenings – obviously to the pub.

Around the Tees, Cameron's Strongarm and the South Durham ales produced at the Castle Eden Brewery enjoyed good reputations.

Often immigrants brought their own diets and dishes with them. The Cornish pasty, as made for the copper miners of Cornwall, could still be found in its traditional form in West Cumberland in the twentieth century.

Chapter Thirteen

LEISURE

It would be difficult to study ancestry in an area like the North Country without reference to leisure pursuits. The reasons for this are twofold. First, it is not beyond the bounds of possibility that some ancestors may have been actively involved in leisure activities at a professional level. Second, even larger numbers were certainly involved at an amateur or semi-professional level or, in the case of spectator sports, as onlookers.

Here, and on the sporting front in particular, loyalty and passion for a team or a club has regularly passed down through a family, even long after that family has moved out of the region. These factors can be seen best at work in association football. The North-East of England has always been a hotbed of this sport, and migrating families have often taken the support of teams such as Newcastle United, Sunderland and Middlesbrough with them. The same applies, to a lesser extent, to professional teams lower down the leagues: Hartlepool, Carlisle United and Darlington.

Though formally in England, Berwick Rangers, interestingly, decided to try its luck in the Scottish League. Up to the middle of the twentieth century, the region had even more league sides with Workington, Barrow and Gateshead prominent; South Shields too had a league team at one point.

Thousands turned out to play in the Saturday and Sunday Leagues, where standards were high and teams such as Blyth Spartans, Crook, West Auckland, Bishop Auckland and Whitley Bay were nationally known.

Cricket has also had great support in the region both on and off the pitch although it was the last decade of the twentieth century before spectators could watch their own first-class county in operation. Prior to the 1990s, county cricket had been played at minor county level in Northumberland, Durham and Cumberland.

Durham, however, had a special reputation for playing the sport from Victorian times onwards and often hosted the national sides of Australia, West Indies, South Africa and India at Sunderland's Ashbrooke ground.

Amateur football team – West Cumbria in the early-twentieth century.

The region has produced many top-class cricketers who have made their mark on first-class county cricket while the local leagues, which stretch into North Yorkshire and North Lancashire, have always been strong.

Today Durham's Riverside ground hosts first-class county, international and test matches.

Rugby too has always had its keen players and spectators. West Cumbria has long been **Rugby League** territory with Barrow, Workington and Whitehaven all having enjoyed national success in the twentieth century. Amateur rugby league has been historically strong too in this part of the region.

Rugby Union has had a foothold since its very early days: a number of clubs have been in existence for well over 125 years. Newcastle's Gosforth Club (part parent to the modern professional Newcastle Falcons), West Hartlepool, Hartlepool Rovers, Durham City and Aspatria are but a few of the sides which have entered the national history books over the years.

The public and private schools in the region have also stood out on the rugby field, providing both international players and captains. Foremost among these schools are Sedbergh, Durham School, Barnard Castle and Newcastle Royal Grammar School. In Wavell Wakefield and Will Carling, Sedbergh School has produced two of England's most successful rugby captains.

Horseracing has also enjoyed a great deal of popular support. The Northumberland Plate, or Pitman's Derby, once held on Newcastle's Town Moor, is now run annually at Newcastle Racecourse. The Carlisle Bell has been

Programme for a regional football derby.

NEWCASTLE UNITED versus CARLISLE

The Black 'N' White, 10p

FIRST DIVISI[...]
•
SAT. 14th SE[...]

contested for centuries and the races at Sedgefield, Redcar and Cartmel race-courses are also well attended.

During the mid-nineteenth century, **professional boat racing** drew huge crowds to the banks of the Tyne. Researchers with the surnames Clasper, Chambers or Renforth in their family tree would be advised to look into the history of this sport, as Harry Clasper, Bob Chambers and Jim Renforth were all household names in the North-East in the 1860s and 1870s due to their prowess at rowing. Boat racing also took place on the Wear, Tees and Talkin Tarn near Brampton in Cumbria.

Hunting, ever controversial, was a way of life in many of the region's rural areas, with people in Cumberland, Northumberland and Durham profession-ally involved as huntsmen and keepers of hounds. Cumberland perhaps carries the flag here, where huntsmen such as John Peel and Joe Bowman are still recalled in song. Indeed, a variant of the 'John Peel' tune has survived to become a dance tune, a regimental march and a television advertisement favourite.

Hunter Joe Bowman – remembered in song.

Fishing as a sport rather than a profession had its followers, with many fine fishing rivers in the region including the Eden, Tweed, Tyne and Wear.

Hardy's shop in Alnwick gained an international reputation for selling fishing tackle, and nineteenth-century Tyneside agricultural merchant Joseph Liddell fished most of the rivers in the North-East, keeping a coded record of catches in his diaries.

Boxing, greyhound racing, motor-cycle racing and quoits also have had their long-term devotees.

For many in the region, leisure time also meant visits to the theatre (and later the cinema) and the music hall. In fact the North-East, and Tyneside in particular, was as much a birthplace of the **music hall** as London itself, although the term 'concert hall' was more commonly applied in the Newcastle area. During the 1860s, the concert halls of Tyneside were awash with local singer-songwriters, their songs of interest to both the social historian and the genealogist as they often mentioned real people.

There is nothing particularly new about this. Elsewhere in the region – in the old county of Cumberland, for instance – there had been songwriters writing about their communities for some time. Robert Anderson (1770–1833) was born in poverty in Carlisle, worked in the weaving trade and wrote about life in the city and the surrounding north Cumbrian rural community. He described the social scene, the building of the clay daubins, or homes, and the merry nights, the dances, songs and sports. In one well-known song, 'The Caldbeck Wedding', the entire text is about the wedding of local weaver Joe Bewley, and many of the people attending the ceremony are traceable in parish sources.

In the North-East of England, songs and ballads abounded, both in street ballad and book form during the early part of the nineteenth century, but really came into their own with the concert halls of the 1860s.

There were three key songwriters here – Ned Corvan, Joe Wilson and Geordie Ridley. With a number of others, they have left hundreds of songs related to all aspects of Tyneside life and culture. The most famous of them is, of course, 'The Blaydon Races', originally written by Ridley to be performed at a benefit evening for the Tyneside oarsman Harry Clasper.

'The Blaydon Races', which famously mentions the year in which it was written, 1862, is almost a social history in itself – sport, transport, communication, fashion and healthcare are all there, as well as real people. In the song, still sung with lust at Newcastle United fixtures, Ridley refers to himself, Coffee Johnny, Jackie Brown the Bellman and Dr Gibbs, all true-life personalities.

John Peel – remembered in song.

A real person celebrated in local song.

When it came to leisure, audiences came to see Ridley, and other entertainers, in pubs, concert halls and theatres; Balhambra's, mentioned in 'The Blaydon Races', was still operating as a form of music hall in the late-twentieth century. Posters and advertisements show that this form of entertainment was equally popular in most of the North-Eastern towns and villages, even in the smaller pit communities.

The theatres were centres for all forms of entertainment – the Empire Theatre in Sunderland, the Theatre Royal in Newcastle, and Her Majesty's Theatre in Carlisle are just a few examples.

The Tyne Theatre in Newcastle was also popular in Victorian times and remains a fine example of a nineteenth-century theatre. The diarist Liddell makes a number of references to family visits there when plays and pantomimes were all the rage.

Earlier in the nineteenth century, the entertainment often came to the consumer, and both travelling fairs and shows were the pick of the day, blazing a trail from central Scotland down into Yorkshire.

On the eastern side of the Pennines, ancestors flocked to watch the shows of the multi-talented Billy Purvis. A typical immigrant (born in Scotland yet raised in the very heart of industrial Newcastle), Purvis was a serious actor, director, clown, musician, conjuror and puppeteer. He appeared with his show at fairs, races, and often in permanent theatres, and was a local legend from the time of the Napoleonic Wars until his death in Hartlepool in the 1850s. So successful was Purvis that statues of various sizes were made and sold to an adoring public.

Purvis also played the Northumbrian pipes, as did a number of rural Northumbrians. He also had a counterpart, not quite as renowned, on the west coast. He was Jimmy McKenny and had a reputation for literally drumming up custom. Theatres continued their success into the twentieth century, when the

Her Majesty's Theatre, Carlisle, now demolished.

cinema developed. Here, Hollywood legend Stan Laurel can claim personal roots which go back into the theatres and cinemas of South Cumbria, Modern County Durham and Wearside.

Finding More

As material relating to leisure tends to be scattered far and wide, it is probably best to offer general advice based on a few examples here.

Both professional and amateur sport tends to produce its own keen writers and historians and, in the event of family researchers discovering medals or photographs relating to a North Country sporting ancestor, amateur or professional, the chances of finding out more about them is quite good. Typical of this kind of sports book is *To Ashbrooke and Beyond*, a well-researched and weighty tome produced in the 1960s covering rugby, cricket, tennis, bowls, hockey and athletics at Sunderland's main amateur sports ground. It is packed with names and details going back to the mid-Victorian era.

Equally detailed is Clive Crickmer's late-twentieth-century history of South Shields Cricket Club. Yet again, names are there in abundance, as they are in Paul Harrison's *The Lads In Blue*, published in 1995 and rightfully claiming, as it did at the time, to be 'the complete history of Carlisle United'.

If there is a cricketer in the family who has played one or more games classified as first-class (and these might be while appearing for Northumberland, Cumberland or Durham), then they are likely to turn up in the extremely thorough *Who's Who of Cricketers*. Local examples here include Alan Townsend, from Stockton-on-Tees, who played 340 games for Warwickshire in the years after the Second World War, and D C H Townsend, from Norton on Tees. He managed to play three times for England in the 1930s although his 'county cricket' was for minor county Durham.

Boat racing is another sport that can be easily researched by reference to newspapers of the mid-Victorian period (see appendixes, Research Guide). Many of the rowers also appear in songs and ballads of the day and there are collections of material relating to Tyneside boat racing in the archives of Newcastle Central Library.

Documents relating to leisure fishing and, in particular, fishing rights, turn up quite frequently in archives, often in papers handed over by solicitors. This is certainly the case with the Northumberland archives and some of those in Cumbria.

Books like the huge Allan's *Tyneside Songs* (1891 edition) have often been reprinted and contain details of many of the local Victorian poets and song-writers; they also contain songs and ballads about real people, and not merely the rich and famous.

Flesh on the Bones

Most of the major sports clubs keep memorabilia, which may be on display or tucked away in a cupboard in the boardroom and can be produced on request. Photographs, in particular, seem to have survived well here and are often displayed on clubhouse walls.

As regards football, Sunderland Museum and Art Gallery has a case dedicated to local footballing heroes Raich Carter and Bobby Gurney. The 'Coaltown' experience at Woodhorn, Ashington, recalls contributions made to the national game by the local Charlton and Milburn families.

The Stephenson Museum celebrates an engine named after legendary Newcastle centre-forward Jackie Milburn. The Newcastle Story in the Discovery Museum charts Newcastle United's progress over the years.

At Newcastle's Centre For Life, the DNA of the border Robson family has received special scrutiny recently. This family, famous for its reiving in years past, has made a major contribution to English football in recent times.

At the Dock Museum in Barrow-in-Furness, some of the successes of the local rugby league side are featured.

References to the role of boat racing appear in Newcastle's Discovery Museum.

The Chantry Bagpipe Museum in Morpeth is worth a visit and has already proved useful to family historians surprised to find ancestors recorded there.

Morpeth's Chantry Bagpipe Museum.

Displays are dedicated to musical individuals from the infamous Jemmy Allen through John Dunn, Robert and James Reid to Jack Armstrong and Tom Clough, and many ordinary folk from the region made names for themselves through the playing of the pipes.

Alnwick, a few miles further north, is home to the unusual House of Hardy Museum, which pays homage to the sport of angling. Hardy's is still a functional business and the museum, opened in the 1980s, consists of exhibits lent by the company's many devotees round the world and by the Hardy family itself. The Hardy Brothers concern, which started in the late-nineteenth century (initially as gunsmiths), still enjoys a world-wide reputation for rods and reels. The first Hardy 'Perfect' reel was patented back in 1891.

An ambitious Museum of Music Hall was opened up in Sunderland in the late-twentieth century but fell victim to financial cuts. Some of the material from it can still be seen in the Discovery Museum at Newcastle. The Museum of Hartlepool has a fine collection of ephemera relating to nineteenth-century leisure in the area.

Many towns and cities have thorough and entertaining histories of their theatres and cinemas; William Gibbon's booklet on Barrow-in-Furness stands as a fine example of such a work (see the Bibliography).

Section Three

MOVEMENT

Chapter Fourteen

MOVEMENT

The industrial revolution (some may argue revolutions) of the eighteenth and nineteenth centuries brought about huge movements in population. With the North Country's heavy involvement in these changes, it is hardly surprising to see immigration and emigration occurring on a large scale. The story of our North Country ancestors would therefore be incomplete without reference to their movements and some examination of the reasons behind them.

Thankfully, the great days of immigration and emigration matched a simultaneous improvement in public record-keeping, which enables modern family historians (aided by current technology), to retrace many of these movements with relative ease.

Immigrants

Mining

The increase in both metal mining and coalmining brought considerable movement in population, with the local expansion in iron mining in the late-nineteenth century providing a particularly fruitful and well-documented example worthy of study.

On both sides of the region, the growth of metal manufacture and the development of iron shipbuilding led to an increase in demand for locally mined iron from mid-century onwards. As the iron mines began to expand and processes were adopted which allowed for more use of British iron, the lead, tin and copper mines elsewhere in the British Isles were in trouble, mainly as a result of foreign competition.

Metal miners were true wanderers and their skills interchangeable, so these developments led to an influx of workers into the iron mines of the North-West during the second part of the nineteenth century. Here was a classic case of push and pull.

In the 1860s and 1870s, whole communities uprooted and moved, often in family and friendship groups. This is particularly true of settlements from the declining copper- and tin-mine areas of South-West England.

At first the miners moved from the South-West on their own, leaving family behind; census returns for Devon and Cornwall during this period often have the wife registered as head of the household, married and responsible for the children. As the miners eventually laid down new roots, the families followed, sometimes by rail and sometimes by sea.

The census of 1851, for example, reveals that there were 738 men and boys in the Devon parish of Marytavy. By 1871 there were only 490. Many of these could now be found in Millom in West Cumberland.

In Tywardreath near St Austell in Cornwall, such was the move northwards that its effect on attendance at church and Sunday school was noted in church records.

On his twenty-first birthday in 1907 Millom man Fred Stephens, Cumbrian-born of parents from the South-West, was given a birthday book. Flick through it today and you will come across surnames associated with Devon and Cornwall: Bennett, Date, Doidge, Friend, Horetop, Penrose, Tawton, Tancock, Williams and Youren. The census for 1901 shows that all those named, like Fred, had settled down in Millom.

Metal mining also saw movement taking place inside and across the region – a form of local immigration. The Pennine lead miners and copper miners of the Lake District suffered the pinch as much as did their colleagues in Devon and Cornwall. In their case, the draw across to the West Cumbrian iron-ore mines was a westward one. Thus we find the Swindale family from Nenthead in the Pennines moving into Millom and the Gregg (or Grigg) family from Coniston making a shorter journey in the 1860s.

*Cumbrian marriage –
Devon- and Cornwall-
born.*

There was similar movement into the coalmines of the North-East and the west coast from Cornwall as some miners went for a complete change. Names beginning with the classic Cornish Pen, Pol and Tre start to appear on official documentation, as well as the likes of Youlden or Youldon and Penrose.

In terms of interchangeable skills, the move from metal to coal was not a totally natural one but the similarities were enough to ensure such moves did take place. Coal also drew in workers of all kinds from Scotland, Wales and the rural areas of England (Scotland and Wales also had working mines to attract the workers).

The 1851 census for Washington on Wearside shows the Laird family all born in Scotland and, as in the metal mines, internal movement across the region was not uncommon. Near to the Lairds were the Swaddles, Watsons and Winships, with family born at various places across the North-East, both in Durham and Northumberland.

Transport

With the sea acting as a major 'roadway' throughout most of the region's history, evidence for movement along the maritime routes will come as no surprise. Bad roads made the inhabitants of Dundee and Kings Lynn, for instance, virtual neighbours to those living in North-Eastern ports whereas North-Eastern access to York and Darlington, nearer as the crow flies, was often difficult by road.

On the west coast, Liverpool, Fleetwood, Barrow, Whitehaven and the Scottish Solway developed similar links. These contacts led to considerable movement, both for ordinary seamen and for officers and intending officers in the merchant service. A good example of this is a long-term link between the North-Eastern port of South Shields and the Shetland Islands. The Orkneys and Shetlands both had a considerable reputation for producing competent seamen who had worked on fishing boats and whalers as youths.

One history of South Shields, written in the mid-nineteenth century, refers to North-Eastern agents placed at Lerwick, the Shetland capital, with the aim of 'procuring suitable youths'. For these youngsters, the temptation was considerable, often starting with the offer of an apprenticeship and then the taking of the tickets to become mates and masters. South Shields remains an important centre for the gaining of maritime 'tickets' today.

One example of this type of migration links the tiny hamlet of Duncansclett on the Shetland island of Burra with the ports of Tyne and Wear. At Duncansclett, James and Grezzel Pottinger (both of whom died on the island), raised a number of sons. The eldest, George, took his ticket in South Shields in the late-1850s, moved there, captained a clipper called the *Ocean Bride* and was swept overboard off the Downs in 1865. His brother William settled in Sunderland and, after working under sail, delivered some of the top steamers directly from launch to their new owners. Their brother Lawrence was living as a seaman in the Master Mariners' Cottages in South Shields in 1891. Brother James Innes Pottinger took his ticket in South Shields, moved there and died of lung disease, having put ashore at Falmouth in 1876. Brother Walter took his ticket at South Shields and, while captaining a northern vessel, died of fever in Calcutta in 1880. Last of all came Thomas. He took his ticket at Dundee but spent the whole of the 1880s and 1890s captaining colliers from the Tyne, working the British coast and across to Europe. For at least twenty years, Thomas and his family lived in South Shields.

Sir Walter Runciman, politican and shipowner, started in similar circum- stances. He was born in Scotland but his father, an ex-mariner, moved to take up coastguard duties on the Northumberland coast. Walter ran away to sea in his youth, worked his way up to a master, retired through ill health and eventually moved to Tyneside, where he set up the shipbuilding business that was to secure his and his family's future. Alnmouth, Berwick, Spittal, Holy Island, South Shields all feature in Walter's early life; Seahouses, Doxford and Newcastle were all involved with the years of his retirement.

The construction of ports and railways also brought workers flooding into the area, and those with a huge Irish connection in particular. This comes out, in an interesting number of ways, in the poor-law records for the Hartlepool Poor Law Union. The authorities' struggle with the Catholic priest in the 1860s has been referred to elsewhere (see chapter 7, Religion). In addition, the Hartlepool guardians had numerous dealings with poor-law unions in Ireland concerning the return of paupers across the Irish Sea.

Hartlepool also features in one version of a famous song on railways and population movement, which has a line running:

> In Eighteen Hundred and Forty Two
> I moved to Hartlepool from Crewe
> And found myself a job to do
> Working on the Railway.

In Penrith (Cumberland), tussles between the railway workers and the authorities were also recorded in song and much has been written over the years about the Tyneside Irish, whose descendants remain vibrant contributors to life along the river today.

Metal Production and Shipbuilding

Metal manufacture and iron shipbuilding were usually found side by side, a factor which also affected patterns of immigration. Typical of this general movement is the experience of workers in the Barrow-in-Furness area. Here, in the mid-nineteenth century, the iron and steel industry in Barrow itself developed alongside the iron-ore mines at nearby Dalton and the Hodbarrow mines at Millom. 'Metal' Shipbuilding came at a later date.

Job Hughes – in Barrow to 'put in the Bessemers'.

In Barrow, general labour was drawn in from Ireland, Scotland and the English countryside but there was also the need for experience. With the development of new technology as steel came to be preferred to iron, tested metalworkers were drawn in from the Black Country of the Midlands and from Wales. One metalworker, Job Bird Hughes moved from Dudley to Barrow in the 1870s; according to family stories, he came simply 'to put the Bessemers in'.

There were also opportunities for those experienced in the use of machinery, as in cloth production. With the surge of the early industrial revolution over in this industry, this meant for some a move to Barrow from other Lancashire towns such as Blackburn, Bolton and Preston. Many of the iron and steelworkers and their children were later drawn into the shipyards, as their skills were required for building iron vessels.

The Barrow experience was mirrored in West Hartlepool, on the east coast, with its similar port/iron-and-steel/shipbuilding pattern, and in Middlesbrough too.

As with the mines, there was movement within these industries from further north; a recent book entitled *A Sundered Land*, for example, tells the true story of a family drawn into the shipbuilding industry on Wearside from sea-related activity close to the Scottish border.

In the early-Victorian period, Ned Corvan, later to be a professional entertainer in the concert halls, moved from Liverpool and found work as a sailmaker on Tyneside before 'treading the boards'.

A hundred years ago South Shields attracted tradesmen and seamen of many nationalities, from Yemen, Aden, Somalia, Africa, India and Malaysia. Known as the Lascars, they settled in South Shields and their story is a long and interesting one. In the late-twentieth century and early-twenty-first century, immigrants from all over the world came to settle in the region. Newcastle and Middlesbrough now contain many who will have to look to the Asian continent for ancestral roots.

Some Jewish communities were set up in the North as a result of the various pogroms in Eastern Europe in the late-nineteenth century, and victims established themselves in a number of northern towns and cities. Here the stories of the Jewish communities in Sunderland, Gateshead and Newcastle make for particularly interesting reading.

During the First World War, a separate community of Belgian refugees was established at Birtley in County Durham. Named Elisabethville, this community of some 6,000 had its own laws and organisation, and inhabitants worked in a local ordnance factory. There were some intermarriages between Belgians and local people, and descendants can be found today both in Belgium and the United Kingdom.

The Second World War also brought people into the region from Eastern Europe, with a significant number from the Baltic region settling in North Cumbria.

Emigrants

While researchers still living in the region may be looking outwards in search for their roots, there are bound to be others outside the region seeking their

Communal building erected for the 'Birtley Belgians'.

own roots within the North Country. This is hardly surprising, as both economic opportunity and economic necessity were capable of driving North Country folk away from their own native land. Some moved overseas, where the old 'push and pull' theory is to be seen clearly at work, particularly in relation to the various mining communities across the region.

In the nineteenth century, one of the attractions for miners was the opening up of other forms of mining centres in South Africa, Australia, the United States and other parts of the American continent. The historian Terry Coleman points out in his work *Passage To America* that 'miners, which the north-east possessed in abundance, were in demand and had an expertise which was to prove both useful and rewarding'.

In Australia, many settlements bear names which will be easily recognised by anyone with North-East connections, and the move to the gold fields of Australia in the 1850s and 1860s was nicely chronicled by the Tyneside singer-songwriter Ned Corvan. As a professional performer, Corvan drew on the emotions of his audiences with three songs about the Australian goldfields, which brought out both the positive and negative sides of life 'down under'. He brings out the reasons for emigration: poor pay ('when we cannot raise our beer it's time to go away') and bad master–men relations ('masters keep us striking so what must a pitman do').

Some emigrants stayed overseas, while others returned, and there are a number of examples among the local mining communities of families with parents born in Britain, older children in Australia or America and younger children back in the North. The 1871 Alston census, for example, records a local family called Millican with its youngest child born in the USA. The father is recorded as a widower, which may explain the return home.

Emigration was not restricted merely to the nineteenth century and the mining industry. Later members of the Pottinger family (see Transport above) ended up living and working in Peru and Vancouver though born in South Shields of Shetland parents. Agricultural merchant Joseph Liddell had a grand-daughter (born Liddell) who emigrated to Canada in the middle of the twentieth century.

Northumbrian connection with the American Ogles.

At an even earlier date, a number of those from the upper classes had emigrated and some of them made significant contributions to the history of the United States. Three eighteenth-century governors of Maryland – Robert Eden, Thomas Bladen and Samuel Ogle – were born in North-East England. Ogle was Northumberland-born. His father was an MP and Ogle (born 1702) joined the army. He became Governor of Maryland and helped to set up horseracing in the state. His home, Bel-air, is still recognised as a classic building.

The Bacon family, from St Bees, contributed to music and trade. William Smallwood, soldier and state governor, was sent back to the family home in Kendal for his education. William Fell, from Ulverston, was Baltimore's first shipbuilder and his family founded the now famous Fell's Point. Robley Duglison, born in Keswick, made a great contribution to American medical history.

As late as the period from 1881 to 1921, when the population of Historic County Durham was still rising, over 125,000 were recorded as lost to the area and officials concluded that 'many probably emigrated overseas'.

In some cases, emigrant families have been keen to keep in touch with their North Country roots. Hylton Castle, now an area of Sunderland, has a castle that stands in its own grounds and has become a focal point for those with the surname Hilton or Hylton. American Hiltons, in particular, appear to have been conscious of recent developments in North-East England and supportive of local efforts to restore the family home. A full-size standard bearing the Hilton colours and family crest was presented to the castle as a token of appreciation for the work done to date 'on behalf of Hiltons everywhere'. It can now be seen flying from the ramparts.

Visitors with the surname Washington or one of its derivatives frequently come to the National Trust Property at Washington Hall on Wearside. Although this manor house passed out of Washington hands at the end of the fourteenth century, it is still considered to be the ancestral home of the family. It later passed into the hands of the Mallory and James families. By the nineteenth century, the house was in decline and used as a tenement block. Restored, it is now a fine example of a northern manor house of the seventeenth century.

There has also been emigration to other parts of the United Kingdom. Movement around Britain has taken place at most points over the past two hundred years, but was particularly noticeable during the slump of the interwar years, which led to a sizeable exit from the North Country.

In Historic County Durham, some migrants were given financial assistance under a Ministry of Labour transference scheme and many seem to have moved to London, the South-East or the Midlands. Light engineering, the car industry and new electrical businesses proved the attraction here. The North Country as a whole began to lose personnel to 'fast-growing, home-market orientated, durable-consumer-goods industries', of which there was little practical experience among the region's employers.

As new towns developed outside the region, this trend continued, leaving Historic County Durham with a net outward migration of 52,300 between 1951 and 1961. Many of those leaving were under forty and took their passionate football support with them! (See chapter 13, Leisure.)

There was also movement within the region: unemployed people in certain North-Eastern urban areas were offered the opportunity of setting up in small-holdings near Wigton, just outside of Carlisle.

Appendixes

RESEARCH GUIDE

Appendix One

ARCHIVES, LIBRARIES AND LOCAL STUDIES CENTRES

There are many significant archive centres and libraries scattered throughout the region and, for the sake of simplicity, the order adopted in the book so far – Cumbria, Northumberland, Tyneside, Wearside, County Durham and Tees Valley – is continued below.

Although researchers often have specifically local needs, it is still advisable for anyone with North Country roots to check out all the major resource centres; the numerous changes made in local governmental arrangements over the years have led to a wide scattering of primary source material. Similarly there is material which has been created at a regional or sub-regional level where committees or organisations covered areas such as 'Tyne and Tees' or 'Northumberland and Durham' or even an entire 'Northern Region'. Yet again it is worth checking all the major centres for such evidence.

It is also worth noting that the growth in interest in genealogy and local history and the increasing availability of heritage grants have combined to ensure a constant updating of facilities and, in some cases, the actual movement or planned movement of archival sites.

Archives

The recommended starting point in every case is what are commonly known as the 'county archives' although some do not fall exactly into the pattern of current county organisation. These archives have been featured frequently in the Finding More sections of each of the main chapters.

In this section too is a guide to resources useful to the family historian, which

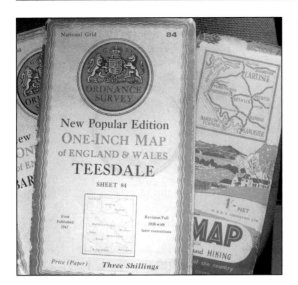

Old maps can help in the tracing of ancestors.

may not have been given extensive space in the main text. These resources include newspapers, trade directories, maps, photographs, illustrations and the records of solicitors and businesses.

Further references to these resources may also be found in the section on libraries and local studies centres.

Cumbria

Since the formation of Cumbria in the 1970s, there have been a number of changes in the way the archive service has been organised in the area. Cumbria now boasts four main centres, in Carlisle, Kendal, Barrow-in-Furness and Whitehaven, and local records tend to rest at the nearest centre (the records for Hodbarrow iron-ore mine, for example, which used to be in Carlisle, can now be found at Barrow-in-Furness near to Millom, site of the former iron-ore mine).

Official documentation notes that 'as a rule of thumb' the records for the former county of Cumberland (with the River Derwent as the dividing line) are to be found at Whitehaven and Carlisle. In Carlisle, original documents from the twelfth century to the present day, relating to the old county north of the River Derwent can be found. These cover the lives of those in and around Carlisle, Keswick and Penrith. Currently these are held at Carlisle Castle but negotiations are under way for a move to larger premises elsewhere in the city.

The Whitehaven repository serves the part of West Cumbria bounded by the River Derwent in the north and the River Duddon in the south. Material

Modern County Durham (see also p. 168)

Like the Tyne and Wear Archives, the Durham County Record Office is a major regional resource, and not merely for the North-East of England. Historic County Durham reached into most of the modern counties developed in the region in recent years and all relevant material produced by the Record Office shows an admirable understanding and concern for the problems this has created. Thus material relating to family history, in particular, is earmarked on the website as having reference to:

- the present county of Durham;
- those areas formerly in County Durham but now part of the areas administered by Gateshead Metropolitan Borough (for example, Winlaton, Ryton, Felling);
- those areas formerly in County Durham but now part of the areas administered by South Tyneside Council (for example, South Shields, Jarrow and Hebburn);
- those areas formerly in County Durham but now part of the areas administered by Sunderland City Council (for example, Sunderland and Silksworth);
- those areas formerly in County Durham but now part of the areas administered by Hartlepool Borough Council (for example, Hartlepool, Seaton Carew) and Stockton Borough Council (for example, Stockton and Norton).

The Borough of Darlington, though no longer officially in the county, seems to have retained its Durham ties more strongly than other places in the Tees Valley, a noteworthy fact for those with Darlington ancestry.

The archive's strong links with the history of mining and the story of the Durham Light Infantry are covered in the relevant chapters.

The historic county's proximity to the former county of Cumberland is also important in terms of some documentation, as is its maintenance of many of the major records relating to the DLI (see appendix 4, Museums and Heritage Centres and chapter 10, Military and Warfare).

DURHAM COUNTY RECORD OFFICE
County Hall, Durham DH1 5UL
Tel: 0191 3833253
Email: record.office@durham.gov.uk
www.durham.gov.uk/recordoffice

Tees Valley (see also p. 168)

Teesside Archives is responsible for collecting and preserving archival material from official and private sources in the areas served by the councils of

Middlesbrough, Redcar and Cleveland, Stockton and Hartlepool.

The Archives keeps many records relating to these local authorities as well as private businesses and solicitors. Business records include those of the owners of the Middlesbrough estate and those of Edward Windross, Master painter, and William Lockwood Taylor, Painter and Decorator, both sets dating from the nineteenth century. Here too are the full and fascinating papers of the Pennyman family of Ormesby Hall.

TEESSIDE ARCHIVES
Exchange House, 6 Marton Road, Middlesbrough TS1 1DB
Tel: 01642 248321
Email: teesside_archives@middlesbrough.gov.uk
www.middlesbrough.gov.uk/ccm/navigation/leisure-and-culture/archives

Other Archives (see also p. 168)

North of England Open Air Museum Regional Resource Centre

Beamish Museum is recommended in the main text as an essential visiting point for those wishing to gain a flavour of life in the North Country, particularly in the North-East, over the last few centuries. Beamish also maintains a Regional Resources Centre with a wealth of material that will be of use and interest to the family historian.

The photographic library contains several hundred photographs of working, home and social life since the invention of the art. Lead mining, iron and steel, transport and other industries are well represented. Photographs are accessible via computer databases in the search room and there are also card indexes.

In addition to the photographs, the centre keeps a number of major collections including the *Durham Advertiser* newspaper, *Agricultural Gazette* and *Farmers' Guardian* and the ICI collection from Teesside, records of the Huwood Mining Machinery Company and stills from BBC Newcastle.

There is a printed book collection of some 64,000 publications covering the last three centuries as well as posters, leaflets, ephemera, prints and maps and some rare nineteenth-century trade catalogues. Many of these are out of print and unavailable elsewhere in the region.

There has also been a campaign to collect oral histories and there are now hundreds of tapes that recount the memories of North-Eastern people through reminiscences, stories, music and song.

The centre is very user-friendly, although it is best to check what is available and when. It is free of charge to researchers on appointment.

The office at Berwick serves an area extending from Berwick, south to Ellingham and across to the Cheviots. Many of the sources are on microfilm only and it is advisable to book a reader beforehand.

The officers at Berwick also have an expertise in tracing cross-border relationships and the office possesses a number of records relating to Scottish ancestry. These archives may be of interest to those with North Cumbrian heritage as well as some with Tyneside ancestry (particularly North Tyneside). They may also be useful to those with ancestry on the Durham/Northumberland border.

Trade directories covering the area in the eighteenth century exist, including a very detailed 1806 directory for Berwick itself, which can be found at the Berwick Record Office.

NORTHUMBERLAND COLLECTIONS SERVICE

Woodhorn, Queen Elizabeth II Country Park, Ashington, Northumberland NE63 9YF
Tel: 01670 528080
Email: collections@woodhorn.org.uk
www.northumberland.gov.uk/collections

BERWICK-UPON-TWEED RECORD OFFICE

Berwick-upon-Tweed Council Office, Wallace Green, Berwick-upon-Tweed TD15 1ED
Tel: 01289 301865
Email: lb@berwick-upon-tweed.gov.uk
www.northumberland.gov.uk/collections
www.berwick-upon-tweed.gov.uk/corp/archives

Tyneside and Wearside (see also p. 168)

The Tyne and Wear Archive Service is housed close to the centre of Newcastle and is in the same building as the Discovery Museum at Blandford House. This is a vital regional and sub-regional facility as it embraces material from Tyneside and Wearside as well as significant evidence relating to Cumbria, Northumberland, Modern County Durham and the Tees Valley.

Material stored at regional or sub-regional level includes the records of medical organisations, such as the British Medical Association's North of England Branch (these cover the last hundred years).

Some of the Trade Union organisations also crossed county boundaries. There are records here, for example, for the Northumberland and Tyne branch of the Amalgamated Society of Woodworkers.

As mentioned in the main text, there are transcripts and indexes for criminal records in Cumberland and Westmorland (1805–1816) and viewers' reports for West Cumbrian coalmines in the early-nineteenth century.

Museum and Archive combined – Blandford House, Newcastle.

This archive is a major centre for family history research, has a helpful website and produces a host of useful leaflets as guides.

The sources mentioned and many other family history sources held by the service are detailed in the booklet *Sources for Family History at Tyne & Wear Archives Service* which is available from the address above or downloadable from the website.

The extensive Tyne and Wear Archives has maps and plans both pre- and post-Ordnance Survey as well as estate maps, some dating back to the seventeenth century. Apprentice records for Gateshead include those for dyers, fullers, locksmiths, blacksmiths, cutlers, joiners and house carpenters from the seventeenth to the nineteenth century.

TYNE AND WEAR ARCHIVES SERVICE
Blandford House, Blandford Square, Newcastle upon Tyne NE1 4JA
Tel: 0191 2326789
Email: via website
www.thenortheast.com and www.archivesnortheast.com

concerning Workington, Cockermouth and Whitehaven is stored here. Records relating to the historic county of Westmorland, and also some for the Sedbergh–Dent district (formerly in the West Riding of Yorkshire) and the Cartmel district (formerly in Lancashire North of the Sands) are to be found at Kendal.

Material concerned with the Furness area and immediate surroundings is in Barrow-in-Furness. In both Barrow and Whitehaven, the Local Studies Libraries are also tied into the Record Offices.

The work of the entire archive service is possibly best approached through its own publication, *Cumbrian Ancestors: Notes for Genealogical Researchers*. This has gone through a number of editions and is an ideal guide for family historians.

In terms of special collections, Kendal also has a number of important named collections. Most significant are the archive of Thomas H Mason, landscape architect of Lancaster and Windermere (late-nineteenth to twentieth centuries), the papers of Lady Anne Clifford of Appleby Castle (1590–1676) and those of Sir Daniel Fleming of Rydal Hall (late-seventeenth century). As Cumbria fringes on both County Durham and Northumberland in the east, those with ancestors on the western fringes of both these counties (in the metal mining areas in particular) may also find material of interest here.

General guides to the Cumbrian Record Offices suggest that Ordnance Survey maps, trade directories, photographs and illustrations are available 'for most areas of Cumbria'; along with local authorities' records and those for civil parishes, landed estates, solicitors, businesses and industries.

The Carlisle office holds local newspapers including the *Carlisle Journal* and *Cumberland Pacquet*. Newspapers on view at Barrow include *Soulby's Ulverston Advertiser* 1848–1914, *Barrow News* 1883–1985 and the *North Western Daily/Evening Mail* 1898–1995; also the *Millom Gazette* 1892-1933. Newspapers at Whitehaven include the *Whitehaven News* and *Cumberland Pacquet*. Newpapers at the Kendal office include the *Westmorland Gazette* and the *Kendal Chronicle/Mercury*.

The adjoining Local Studies Library at Barrow holds books relating to Barrow and the surrounding area, and an extensive collection of periodicals covering Lancashire, Cheshire, Cumberland and Westmorland. It also has a collection of photographs and printed ephemera.

The Local Studies Library at Whitehaven contains an important collection of books, illustrations, journals, reports and other printed and original materials relating to all aspects of life in the area.

CUMBRIA RECORD OFFICE CARLISLE

The Castle, Carlisle CA3 8UR
Tel: 01228 607285
Email: carlisle.record.office@cumbriacc.gov.uk
www.cumbria.gov.uk/archives

CUMBRIA RECORD OFFICE KENDAL
County Offices, Kendal LA9 4RQ
Tel: 01539 773540
Email: kendal.record.office@cumbriacc.gov.uk
www.cumbria.gov.uk/archives

CUMBRIA RECORD OFFICE AND LOCAL STUDIES LIBRARY BARROW-IN-FURNESS
140 Duke Street, Barrow-in-Furness LA 14 1XW
Tel: 01229 894363
Email: barrow.record.office@cumbriacc.gov.uk
www.cumbria.gov.uk/archives

CUMBRIA RECORD OFFICE AND LOCAL STUDIES LIBRARY WHITEHAVEN
Cumbria Record Office and Local Studies Library, Scotch Street, Whitehaven CA 28 7NL
Tel: 01946 852920
Email: whitehaven.record.office@cumbriacc.gov.uk
www.cumbria.gov.uk/archives

It is advisable to check opening hours with individual offices.

Northumberland (see also p. 168)

These are exciting times for family and local historians with an interest in Northumberland, as much of the material from the county archives has recently been moved, reorganised and settled in one place. Previously, it had been kept at two sites: Gosforth, on the northern fringes of Newcastle, and Morpeth. A third site, at Berwick, continues as before.

The new archive site at Woodhorn, near Ashington, is dovetailed in with a modern museum of mining heritage (see appendix 4, Museums and Heritage Centres). It currently headlines itself as The Northumberland Collections Service and the archive area has been specially tailored to accommodate both beginner and seasoned researcher. The archive material has been sorted and stored into pods for ease of access. The material also promises to be among the best-organised in the country. For an entire year, most of the documents now resting here were unavailable while the process of stocktaking, conservation and electronic cataloguing took place. A string of records almost four miles long was involved. Woodhorn boasts a wide range of newspapers connected to Northumberland and other areas in the North-East, and also keeps family and estate papers plus business records.

The library is also home to the Corder manuscripts, a unique collection of thirty-eight complete volumes relating to local topography and family history. These are hand-written and include extensive material on shipbuilding families.

The general user guide at Sunderland Local Studies Centre is particularly helpful, showing newspapers from 1831 'to last night's *Echo*', many of which are well indexed for important events and some local obituaries.

The main libraries at Washington and Houghton-le-Spring also have local material and often host displays with local history and family history researchers in mind (details from the City Library).

CITY OF SUNDERLAND LOCAL STUDIES CENTRE
City Library and Arts Centre, Fawcett Street, Sunderland SR1 1RE
Tel: 0191 514 8439
Email: local.studies@sunderland.gov.uk

Modern County Durham

The libraries' website gives access to four interesting and useful projects mentioned in the main text: the Durham Record, the Durham Miner Project, the Community Heritage Project and the Coal Mining Oral History Project. Libraries also sell a number of local history publications, including those in a popular *Memories* series. Many local history groups meet in the local library.

Durham Clayport Library has the PRO index, censuses for most of the county and a local collection recommended by the county council as being of special importance. It also has a reference section, which holds sources of information about Modern County Durham, especially the northern part.

The local studies collection includes over 10,000 books, pamphlets, articles and newspaper cuttings. Maps are available too, some in original print and others on database. Local newspapers kept here include the *Durham County Advertiser* (1814–1998) and the *Durham Chronicle*. Many branch libraries also keep cuttings and photographs.

DURHAM COUNTY LIBRARIES
County Hall, Durham DH1 5UL
Tel: 0191 383 3000
www.durham.gov.uk/durhamcc/usp.nsf/pws/Libraries+-
+Discover+Local+and+Family+History+Resources

DURHAM CLAYPORT LIBRARY
Millennium Place, Durham City DH1 1WA
Tel: 0191 386 4003
www.durham.gov.uk

Tees Valley

Although, strictly speaking, now in Tees Valley, the Darlington Centre For Local Studies maintains strong links with Modern County Durham and holds records relating to parts of the county past and present.

Stockton too keeps a wide range of material as witnessed by the local library website. The Central Reference Library is the largest in the borough and is particularly proud of its local and family history collections.

Hartlepool too keeps many useful records: parish registers, newspapers such as the local *Mail* and old *South Durham and Cleveland Mercury* plus references to both world wars and, in particular, the bombardment of the Hartlepools in 1914. It has an excellent website linked to those of other ports.

DARLINGTON CENTRE FOR LOCAL STUDIES

Darlington Library, Crown Street, Darlington DL1 1ND
Tel: 01325 349630
Email: localstudies@darlington.gov.uk
www.darlington.gov.uk/Education/Library/Centre+for+Local+Studies

STOCKTON REFERENCE LIBRARY

Stockton Central Library, Church Road, Stockton-on-Tees TS18 1TU
Tel: 01642 528079
Email: reference.library@stockton.gov.uk
www.stockton.gov.uk/citizenservices/leisureandents

HARTLEPOOL REFERENCE LIBRARY,

Central Library, 124 York Road, Hartlepool TS24 9DE
Tel: 01429 263778
Email: infodesk@hartlepool.gov.uk
www.portcities.org.uk/hartlepool

Old Yorkshire Links

MIDDLESBROUGH REFERENCE LIBRARY

Victoria Square, Middlesbrough TS1 2AY
Tel: 01642 729001
Email: reference_library@middlesbrough.gov.uk
www.middlesbrough.gov.uk

REDCAR REFERENCE LIBRARY

Coatham Road, Redcar TS10 1RP
Tel: 01642 472162
Email: redcar_library@redcar-cleveland.gov.uk
www.redcar-cleveland.gov.uk/libraries

MORPETH LIBRARY
Gas House Lane, Morpeth, Northumberland NE61 1TA
Tel: 01670 534514
www.northumberlandlibraries.com

Tyneside

The Local Studies and Family History Centre in the Central Library lies close to the main shopping centre in Newcastle and deals with all aspects of documentation about the city and people who lived there.

The coverage of some of the material also extends further, into Northumberland, Durham and Cumbria. A leaflet, *Local Studies Library Genealogy Guide Number 2: Genealogical Sources*, describes sources available in detail and can be downloaded from the library website.

Other libraries on Tyneside also have their own highly useful and well-staffed local studies centres. The Local Studies Centre at Gateshead Central Library has a wide range of material, with sport, tradition and the Belgian immigrants featuring highly.

North Shields and South Shields too have useful local history collections.

Gateshead Local Studies Library has past copies of the *Gateshead Observer*. North Shields has an index to the *Shields Daily News* from 1864 to 1960, partial indexes to other papers and a series of cuttings and notes on local families.

South Shields possesses copies of the *Shields Gazette* as well as national indexes. It also has a large photographic collection comprising of over 10,000 historical photographs of the local area, shipping, war damage and the Jarrow March collection.

NEWCASTLE UPON TYNE CENTRAL LIBRARY
Local Studies/Family History, Princess Square, Newcastle upon Tyne NE99 1DX
Tel: 0845 002 0336
Email: local.studies@newcastle.gov.uk (information@newcastle gov.uk – 2007/8 closed for rebuilding)
www.newcastle.gov.uk/libraries

GATESHEAD CENTRAL LIBRARY
Prince Consort Rd, Gateshead NE8 4LN
Tel: 0191 433 8430
Email: anthealang@gateshead.gov.uk
www.gateshead.gov.uk/ls

NORTH TYNESIDE CENTRAL LIBRARY
Local Studies Centre, Northumberland Square, North Shields NE30 1QU
Tel: 0191 200 5424
Email: local.studies@northtyneside.gov.uk
www.northtyneside.gov.uk/libraries

SOUTH TYNESIDE CENTRAL LIBRARY
Prince George Square, South Shields NE33 2PE
Tel: 0191 427 1818
Email: localstudies.library@s-tyneside-mbc.gov.uk
www.s-tyneside-mbc.gov.uk

Wearside

Because Wearside constitutes the modern City of Sunderland, the Local Studies Centre at the Central Library is crucial to genealogical research. The centre is well equipped for family history research and has a number of useful guided leaflets and material out on the open shelves. There are also local history leaflets on the Victoria Hall Disaster, Jack Crawford, shipbuilding on the Wear and more. This centre is well stocked and knowledgeably staffed. It is also situated conveniently close to the railway/metro station and the city's museum.

Guides like this are becoming more common.

**BEAMISH, THE NORTH OF ENGLAND OPEN AIR MUSEUM
REGIONAL RESOURCE CENTRE**
Beamish, County Durham DH9 0RG
Tel: 0191 370 4000
Email: museum@beamish.org.uk
www.beamish.org.uk

Northumberland and Durham Family History Society Research Centre

The research centre describes itself as 'very much DIY' and is placed conveniently close to Newcastle Central Station.The material kept there covers most of North-East England with the counties named being taken in their historic context.

The centre has a fiche room with census material, poll books, national probate indexes and directories.

The library has books on a wide range of subjects. A recent leaflet lists the following topics: census, nonconformists, local history, Who's Who, education, family trees and histories, general reference and overseas research, Armed Forces, Wills and Admonitions, exchange journals and parish transcripts of baptisms, marriages, burials, cemetery records and monumental inscriptions.

The society welcomes visitors and recommends that some form of financial contribution be made.

**NORTHUMBERLAND AND DURHAM FAMILY HISTORY SOCIETY
RESEARCH CENTRE**
2nd Floor, Bolbec Hall, 23, Westgate Rd, Newcastle upon Tyne NE1 1SE
Tel: 0191 2612159
Email: researchcentre@ndfhs.org.uk
www.ndfhs.org.uk

The National Archives

In addition to the many documents referred to in the text, holdings at TNA include some useful material in the COAL series; railway company and staff records are in RAIL and AN (British Rail); and military service records to *c*.1920 are in ADM, AIR, WO respectively.

THE NATIONAL ARCHIVES
Kew, Richmond, Surrey, TW9 4DU
Tel: 020 8876 3444.
Contact: www.nationalarchives.gov.uk/contact/form
www.nationalarchives.gov.uk

Libraries and Local Studies Centres

These include details to resources useful to the family historian which may not have been referred to in the main text, such as newspapers, trade directories, maps, photographs, illustrations, solicitors' and business records. Some of these may also be found in the Archives section.

Cumbria

Past newspapers can be found in the six main libraries in Cumbria: Carlisle, Kendal, Whitehaven, Workington, Penrith and Barrow-in-Furness. Many of them have been microfilmed and indexed. In some cases, the libraries also have census material. In some instances, as mentioned above, the local studies centres in libraries are tied into the county archival system. The address below is for details on the various main libraries in the county mentioned in the main text.

CUMBRIA LIBRARY SERVICES
Cumbria Libraries HQ, Arroyo Block, The Castle, Carlisle, Cumbria CA3 8UR
Tel: 01228 607295
Email: information@cumbriacc.gov.uk
www.cumbria.gov.uk

Northumberland

All branch libraries in Northumberland have reference and lending collections containing core local-studies titles and stock relevant to their area. Larger libraries have developed strengths in particular area of local studies, for example shipbuilding at Blyth and family history at Hexham.

At Blyth Local Studies Library, there are local newspapers from 1874 and some trade directories; local newspapers and trade directories are kept at Hexham Local Studies Library.

Most of the material kept at Morpeth has now been transferred to the new facility at Woodhorn, although there is some census material and also local history books, which have now been placed in the loan system.

BLYTH LIBRARY
Blyth Library, Bridge Street, Blyth, Northumberland NE24 2DJ
Tel: 01670 361352
www.northumberlandlibraries.com

HEXHAM LIBRARY
Queen's Hall, Beaumont Street, Hexham, Northumberland NE46 3LS
Tel: 01434 652488
www.northumberlandlibraries.com

Both reference libraries have excellent websites with reference to material available and publications of use to the family historian.

Other Libraries

Newcastle University Library is equipped for academic research but has a number of important special collections relating to the history of the North-East. The university's Robinson Library has unique special collections relating to the North-East, mainly covering the eighteenth to twentieth centuries. Although they are intended mainly to support teaching and academic work, they do contain material of interest to the genealogist and the FARNE (Folk Archive Resource North East) research network is online and easy to use (see appendix 2, Web Resources).

NEWCASTLE UNIVERSITY LIBRARY (Robinson Library)
Newcastle University Library, NE2 4HQ, United Kingdom.
Tel: 0191 222 7662
Email: lib-readerservices@ncl.ac.uk
www.ncl.ac.uk/library/

Durham University has many records associated with the widely spread diocese of Durham, including Bishops' Transcripts and marriage-licence applications, wills proved in the Durham Consistory Court 1540–1857 and private papers. A leaflet, *A Brief guide to the chief series of records of genealogical interest in the University Library*, can be downloaded from the site.

ARCHIVES AND SPECIAL COLLECTIONS, UNIVERSITY OF DURHAM
Durham University Library, Palace Green, Durham DH1 3RN
Tel: 0191 3342932
www.dur.ac.uk/library/asc

Durham Cathedral Library has a massive collection of material, mostly concentrating on the cathedral itself.

DURHAM CATHEDRAL LIBRARY
The College, Durham DH1 3EH
Tel: 0191 386 2489
Email: Library@durhamcathedral.co.uk
www.dur.ac.uk/cathedral.library

Newcastle Literary and Philosophical Society is the oldest of its kind; the 'Lit and Phil' has a massive and ever increasing library of information related to all aspects of life and work in Newcastle, on Tyneside and, indeed, relating to most of the region. It has connections with most of the famous Tynesiders:

George Stephenson demonstrated his safety lamp here, and Joseph Swan his electric light bulb. This is a membership club and is particularly renowned for its collection of material on traditional music and musicians of the North-East.

THE LITERARY AND PHILOSOPHICAL SOCIETY OF NEWCASTLE UPON TYNE

23, Westgate Road, Newcastle upon Tyne NE1 1SE
Tel: 0191 2320192
Email library@litandphil.org.uk
www.litandphil.org.uk

The massive potential of modern technology ensures that things move on apace. From summer 2007 a new venture on the part of Museums Libraries Archives North East (MLA) promises to offer a 'professional archive research service . . . without setting foot outside your front door'. In the future this will probably be the starting point for any North-East archival research. The service can be reached via www.thenortheast.com or www.archivesnortheast.com. These sites may, in time, make other North-East-related sites redundant.

Appendix Two

WEB RESOURCES

T he fast speed at which technology develops has led to a mass of useful information becoming available across the Internet. Those sites (especially related to museums, libraries and archives) that have already been listed in the appropriate place are not repeated below.

In some cases, the content is so large that the meagre references here hardly do them justice; they are often storehouses of information about where to look as well as providers of useful factual information.

At the same time, seasoned researchers rightly advise those setting out on the path of family history for the first time to get as close to the original material as possible by actually visiting the resource centres; this is sound advice.

Among the many sites available, the following come recommended:

www.wellinever.info and www.nemlac.co.uk give access to a number of other relevant sites and a wealth of information about the history of the North-Eastern part of the region. (NEMLAC is the North-East Museums, Libraries and Archives Council). This is a real goldmine of advice and information.

www.northeastengland.talktalk.net is a site with wide coverage of many aspects of North-Eastern life, including articles on the history of the area and an interactive map with placename meanings, local history and details of access to further material.

www.thenortheast.com connects to national and local government departments, and also links to attractions, museums and what's on in the North-East. It has sections on history and museums and also allows searching of a database of prominent local newspapers. Developing a key role from 2007.

www.tomorrowshistory.com is a web-based regional local-studies resource for North-East England with links to libraries, museums, archives and record offices, plus local and community groups.

www.genuki.org.uk is a gateway to genealogical information on the North-East and Cumbria, as well as other parts of the country.

www.a2a.pro.gov.uk is the English strand of the UK archives network 'providing over 1,000 years of documentary heritage online'. 'Picks and Pistons', which is available on this site, features about 13,000 pages of catalogues recording many aspects of industrial history but keying coal, railway, ships, iron and steel.

An excellent guide to the site is available from the three major archive services in the North-East, and many of the major library and archive resources in the region are catalogued here.

www.dmm.org.uk is the Durham Miners' website. It covers the history of mining in the North-East of England and contains a searchable database of miners killed in colliery accidents.

www.genuki.org.uk/big/eng/ncl covers trade directory holdings in northern libraries.

www.twmuseums.org.uk/memorynet is known simply as MemoryNet. This is a new site capturing memories and experiences of communities linked with the sea. Its early work involved input from North and South Shields, Tynemouth, Saltburn, Cullercoats and Sunderland.

www.bpears.org.uk/NE-Diary An excellent site prepared by Roy Ripley and Brian Pears, which covers North-Eastern life in the Second World War.

http://www.asaplive.com/FARNE/home.cfm is the Folk Archive Resource North East. This is a fascinating site which covers everything to do with traditional music, song and dance across the North-East. It also has photographs and contains a surprising amount of material useful to the family historian.

www.imagine.org.uk The name stands for Images Museums And Galleries In the North-East and the site gives a good impression of collections of historic material available in the north-east of the region.

www.roughfellsheep.co.uk gives an insight into all to do with the history and practice of sheep farming in the Rough Fell area of Cumbria.

http://www.lakestay.co.uk/shipbuild.html An interesting site which deals with shipbuilding in Whitehaven.

http://www.northpennineancestors.co.uk Extremely well organised for all interested in ancestors from the borders of the Pennine counties. Very good on mining.

http://communities.northumberland.gov.uk/ Award-winning site covering the whole county and of massive use to family history researchers. The council's own account of the site is fully descriptive.

> The Northumberland Communities website contains a range of learning resource material that reflects Northumberland's heritage, providing a base for studying the County's history. The website provides a starting point for understanding the development of communities in Northumberland. It also seeks to illustrate the range of sources for family and local history research that are available via Northumberland Archives Service.

Beneath this explanation on the site is a list of over seventy communities featured on the site, from Wark-on-Tweed in the north down to Seaton Sluice on the coast, and across to Haltwhistle on the Cumbrian border.

www.teessideonline.net/kb.php?mode=article&k=23 covers many aspects of heritage in the Tees Valley.

There are also a number of useful websites referring to Hartlepool:
www.hartlepool-sthilda.org.uk
www.hms-trincomalee.co.uk
Deal with sea-based communities in the North-East and common heritage-booklet published for the Year of the Sea in 2005.

www.dormanmuseum.co.uk/stories/index.htm Contains eye-witness accounts of the Second World War in and around Middlesbrough.

The following wider websites will also prove useful:
www.24hourmuseum.org.uk
www.1901censusonline.com
www.ancestry.co.uk
www.armymuseums.co.uk
www.cyndislist.com
www.familyhistoryonline.net
www.thegenealogist.co.uk
www.genuki.org.uk
www.ncm.org.uk
www.parishchest.com

See also p. 168 and the significance of www.archivesnortheast.com

Appendix Three

OTHER USEFUL ORGANISATIONS AND RESOURCES

CUMBRIA FAMILY HISTORY SOCIETY
www.cumbriafhs.com

Check the website for latest contact addresses. This is a very active society and produces a quarterly newsletter. The publishing programme includes many items, in particular the 1851 census. Quarterly meetings are held in a number of towns around the County, in Manchester, and in London. The Society is a member of the Federation of Family History Societies, the North West Group of Family History Societies and a founder member of the Friends of Cumbria Archives.

NORTHUMBERLAND AND DURHAM FAMILY HISTORY SOCIETY
2nd Floor, Bolbec Hall, 23, Westgate Rd, Newcastle upon Tyne NE1 1SE
Tel: 0191 262 2159
www.ndfhs.org.uk

See details in the Archives section.

THE HERITAGE CENTRE, BELLINGHAM
Station Yard, Woodburn Road, Bellingham NE48 2DF
Tel: 01434 220050
www.bellingham-heritage.org.uk

Situated in the old station yard, this facility is geared to the ancestral researcher with reiver blood. Here there is 'a huge computerised photographic archive and a family/history/genealogy database'.

FRIENDS OF SUNDERLAND OLD PARISH CHURCH
(THE RECTOR GRAY SOCIETY)
www.rootsweb.com/~fosopc

The website should provide current contact details. The Society is dedicated to the protection of all to do with 'Old' Sunderland (the East End) from the eighteenth century to the twentieth century. The site hosts events connected to local family history.

FRIENDS OF HOUGHTON HILLSIDE CEMETERY
Detached churchyard of St Michael and All Angels Church, Sunderland Street, Houghton-le Spring.
www.houghton-hillside-cemetery.org.uk

See the website for current details. This is an important resource for anybody with ancestry in Houghton and is mentioned in the main text (see chapter 7, Religion). The society is extremely proactive in all aspects of local and family history and, in particular, reviving the cemetery and its records.

LIVING HISTORY NORTH EAST
West Wear Street, Sunderland SR2 1 XD
Tel: 0191 565 1566

This is a voluntary organisation financed by a number of official bodies and is an oral history unit dedicated to the collection of living memory on audio and video-tape. This includes to date memories of wartime captivity and twentieth-century pit disasters. Permanent home in the offing and welcomes family historians' interest.

CHURCHES CONSERVATION TRUST
1, West Smithfield, London EC1A 9EE
Tel: 020 7213 0660
Email: central@tcct.org.uk
www.visitchurches.org.uk

St Andrew, Bywell and St Andrew, Shotley, in Northumberland; St Stephen's Tower, Low Elswick, in Newcastle, and Holy Trinity, Sunderland are all closed churches accessed through this organisation.

Appendix Four

MUSEUMS AND HERITAGE CENTRES

All these centres are useful for putting flesh on ancestral bones and there is always a chance that material referring to specific ancestors may turn up in one of them.

Cumbria

THE DOCK MUSEUM, BARROW-IN-FURNESS
North Road, Barrow-in-Furness LA14 2PW
Tel: 01229 876400
Email: dockmuseum@barrowbc.gov.uk
www.dockmuseum.org.uk

Covers shipbuilding and all aspects of working and social life in the Furness area.

MUSEUM OF LAKELAND LIFE AND INDUSTRY
Abbot Hall, Kendal, LA9 5AL
Tel: 01539 722464
www.lakelandmuseum.org.uk

Features work, daily life and entertainment over the last three centuries.

FARFIELD MILL ARTS AND HERITAGE CENTRE
Garsdale Road, Sedbergh LA 10 5LW
Tel: 01539 621958
Email: themanager@farfieldmill.org
www.farfieldmill.org

Deals with the history of wool industry in the area.

CUMBERLAND PENCIL MUSEUM
Southey Works, Keswick, Cumbria CA12 5NG
Tel: 01768 773626
Email: museum@acco-uk.co.uk
www.pencils.co.uk

Describes the discovery of graphite and the production of pencils in the town.

KESWICK MUSEUM AND ART GALLERY
Fitz Park, Station Road, Keswick CA12 4NF
Tel: 01768 73263
Email:keswick.museum@allerdale.gov.uk

Deals with the move of Keswick from mining centre to tourist town.

PENRITH MUSEUM
Robinson's School, Middlegate, Penrith CA11 7PT
Tel: 01768 865105
Email: museum@eden.gov.uk

Located in a listed building and encompassing many aspects of local history.

HELENA THOMPSON MUSEUM
Park End Road, Workington CA14 4DE
Tel: 01900 606155
E-mail: whghtm@hotmail.co.uk

Focuses on mining, shipbuilding and the iron and steel industries associated with the town.

THE EDWARD HAUGHEY SOLWAY AVIATION MUSEUM
Aviation House, Carlisle Airport, Carlisle CA6 4NW
Tel: 01228 573823
Email: info@solway-aviation-museum.co.uk
www.solway-aviation-museum.co.uk

A developing museum – contact for opening times.

HAIG COLLIERY MINING MUSEUM
Solway Road, Kells, Whitehaven Cumbria CA28 9BG
Tel: 01946 599949
Email: museum@haig1.freeserve.co.uk

Exhibits winding engines, headgear and coalmining memorabilia.

THE WORDSWORTH TRUST
Dove Cottage, Grasmere, Cumbria LA22 9SH
Tel: 01539 435544
www.wordsworth.org.uk

Has links with the poet but also eighteenth-century Lakeland life.

MARYPORT MARITIME MUSEUM
1, Senhouse Street, Maryport CA15 6AB
Tel: 01900 813738
Email: maryport.maritime.museum@allerdale.gov.uk
www.allerdale.gov.uk/maryport-maritime-museum

Maryport's maritime past.

Reminders of maritime heritage.

THE BEACON
West Strand, Whitehaven, Cumbria CA28 7LY
Tel: 01946 592302
www.thebeacon-whitehaven.co.uk

Covers the town's industrial, social and maritime past and its transatlantic links.

CARLISLE CASTLE
The Castle, Carlisle, Cumbria CA3 8UR
Tel: 01228 591922
www.english-heritage.org.uk

Useful for detailed information on the Jacobite Rebellions, and the Forty-five in particular.

BORDER AND KING'S OWN BORDER REGIMENTAL MUSEUM
Queen Mary's Tower, The Castle, Carlisle, Cumbria CA3 8UR
Tel: 01228 532774
Email: borderregiment@aol.com and korbrmuseum@aol.com
www.kingsownbordermuseum.btik.com

Tells the complete regimental history.

TULLIE HOUSE MUSEUM AND ART GALLERY CARLISLE
Castle Street, Carlisle, Cumbria CA3 8TP
Tel: 01228 534781
www.tulliehouse.co.uk
Email: enquiries@tulliehouse.co.uk

The story of city and border life with a leaning towards the days of the reivers.

THE RUM STORY
Lowther Street, Whitehaven, Cumbria CA28 7DN
Tel: 01946 592933
www.rumstory.co.uk
Email:info@rumstory.co.uk

Illustrates maritime life, smuggling and slavery.

HONISTER SLATE MINE
Honister Pass, Borrowdale, Keswick, Cumbria
Tel: 01768 777230
www.honister.com

Based on caverns hacked out by Victorian miners for the extraction of green slate.

NENTHEAD MINES HERITAGE CENTRE
Nenthead, Alston CA9 3PD
Tel: 01434 382037
www.npht.com
Email: info@npht.com

Tells the story of the once successful lead and zinc mining industry in the area.

ESKDALE MILL
Boot, Holmrook CA19 1TG
Tel: 01946 723335
www.visitcumbria.com/wc/eskmill.htm

A cornmill with two wheels, dating back to the sixteenth century.

FLORENCE MINE HERITAGE CENTRE
Florence Mine, Egremont CA22 2NR
Tel: 01946 825830
Email: info@florencemine.co.uk
www.florencemine.co.uk

Has a mock drift in the museum and covers Cumbria's extractive industries.

Northumberland

BERWICK BOROUGH MUSEUM
The Clock Block, Berwick Barracks Parade, Berwick-upon-Tweed TD15 1DQ
Tel: 01289 301869
www.discovertheborders.uk/places

Describes all aspects of life in Berwick and district from mining to garrisoning.

KING'S OWN SCOTTISH BORDERERS MUSEUM
The Barracks, The Parade, Berwick-upon-Tweed TD15 1DG
Tel: 01289 307 426
www.kosb.co.uk/museum

Displays uniforms, badges, medals etc. from 1689 to the present day.

HEATHERSLAW CORN MILL

Ford & Etal Estates, Ford, Northumberland TD15 2QA
Tel: 01890 820488
Email: tourism@ford-and-etal.co.uk
www.ford-and-etal.co.uk

A nineteenth-century undershot mill for the milling of wheat.

GRACE DARLING MUSEUM

Radcliffe Road, Bamburgh NE 69 7AE
Tel: 01668 214465
www.discovertheborders.co.uk/places

Refurbished and reopening in 2007 with a great deal more on Grace Darling and lifeboat activity.

Grace Darling – Northumberland heroine.

BERWICK PARISH CHURCH

Holy Trinity – guided tours can be arranged with the vicar (see updated local tourist guide).

BERWICK TOWN WALLS

Encircling the old town and open all year round.
Tel: 01289 330733

PRESTON TOWER

Chathill
Tel: 01665 589227

One of the few surviving pele towers, open all year round.

MUSEUM OF ANTIQUITIES

Alnwick Castle, Alnwick NE66 2NQ
Tel: 01665 510777
www.alnwickcastle.com

Alnwick Castle – remains up to medieval times – mostly associated with the Percy family.

BAILIFFGATE MUSEUM

14, Bailiffgate, Alnwick NE66 1LX
Tel: 01665 605847
Email.ask@bailiffgatemuseum.co.uk
www.bailiffgatemuseum.co.uk

This is the local history museum for Alnwick and district and is situated in a former church. The museum invites visitors to investigate their heritage in the 'ever expanding research area'.

FUSILIERS MUSEUM OF NORTHUMBERLAND

The Abbot's Tower, Alnwick Castle, Alnwick NE66 1NG
Tel: 01665 602152
Email: fusnorthld@aol.com
www.northumberlandfusiliers.org.uk

The museum is an independent charitable trust and a campaign is under way to enhance the website and the collection with heritage lottery funding. The history of the Regiment is told in chronological order via the use of story panels and pictures and relevant artefacts.

WOODHORN
QE II Country Park, Ashington NE63 9YF
Tel: 01670 528080
www.experiencewoodhorn.com

Brand-new facility with much relating to the local colliery – part of the new complex contains most of the Northumberland archives.

CHANTRY BAGPIPE MUSEUM
Bridge Street, Morpeth NE61 1PD
Tel 01670 500717
www.bagpipemuseum.org.uk

Set in the listed thirteenth-century Chantry Bridge Chapel. Features bagpipes and pipers from round the world, with a special eye to Northumberland.

CHERRYBURN: THOMAS BEWICK'S BIRTHPLACE
Mickley, Stocksfield NE43 7DD
Tel: 01661 843276
www.nationaltrust.org.uk

The famous engraver, artist and naturalist was born in this cottage in the mid-eighteenth century – of interest to anybody with roots in rural Northumberland about this time.

GEORGE STEPHENSON'S BIRTHPLACE
Street House, Wylam-on-Tyne NE41 8BP
Tel: 01661 853457
www.nationatrust.org.uk

A 1760s coalmining tenement furnished to represent the time of Stephenson's birth 1781.

HEXHAM OLD GAOL
Hallgate, Hexham NE46 3NH
Tel: 01434 652349
www.tynedale.gov.uk

One of the earliest purpose-built prisons in the country: 'The collection of objects, photographs, documents, books and music will help you explore local and family history.'

WYLAM RAILWAY MUSEUM
Falcon Centre, Falcon Terrace, Wylam NE41 8EE
Tel: 01661 852174

A small museum relating to Wylam's special place in railway history, with links to Hedley, Stephenson and Hackworth.

HOUSE OF HARDY FISHING MUSEUM
Willowburn, Alnwick NE66 2PF
Tel: 01665 510027
enquiries@houseofhardy.co.uk
www.hardygreys.com

Tyneside

THE DISCOVERY MUSEUM
Blandford House, Blandford Square, Newcastle upon Tyne NE1 4JA
Tel: 0191 2326789
Email: discovery@twmuseums.org.uk
www.twmuseums.org.uk/discovery

An essential place for visitors with Newcastle or Tyneside ancestry and conveniently placed within the same building as the Tyne and Wear Archives – also handy for Newcastle Central Station. See the Newcastle Story, A Soldier's Life and the Story of the Tyne, Working Lives, The Tyneside Challenge and Parsons's famous *Turbinia*.

SOUTH SHIELDS ART GALLERY AND MUSEUM
Ocean Road, South Shields NE33 2JA
Tel: 0191 456 8740
Email: southshields@twmuseums.org.uk/southshields
www.twmuseums.org.uk/southshields

South Shields and district through the ages has links with writer Catherine Cookson, and here can be found the Catherine Cookson Trail.

Catherine Cookson's novels still enjoy huge popularity. They described life in the North-East, particularly in the days of her youth, and still make required reading for anyone with ancestors in working-class Tyneside during that period.

The trail takes the visitor through what is left of historic South Shields and the Tyne Dock area. It also reaches into the villages around which South Shields developed.

The museum and art gallery also features aspects of Catherine Cookson's work although, as the twenty-first century progresses, the theme has moved more towards the history of South Shields and South Tyneside than the life and works of the author.

This said, the hand of the author still lies heavily on the exhibits. There are reconstructions from her childhood home at 10 William Black Street, where she lived in her youth. The gallery also has a reconstruction of Cissie Affleck's shop. Catherine used to play regularly outside this shop and there is a wonderful description of a similar one in *Kate Hannigan*.

STEPHENSON RAILWAY MUSEUM
Middle Engine Lane, North Shields NE29 8DX
Tel: 0191 200 7146
www.twmuseums.org.uk/stephenson

Many exhibits linked to the development of early railways in the North-East

SEGEDUNUM ROMAN FORT BATHS AND MUSEUM
Buddle Street, Wallsend NE28 6HR
Tel: 0191 236 9347
Email: info@twmuseums.org.uk
www.twmuseums.org.uk/segedunum

Not merely a museum for Roman times and has much on Wallsend's industrial heritage.

BOWES RAILWAY
Springwell Village, Gateshead NE9 7QJ
Tel: 0191 416 1847
Email: Railway Secretary (see website)
www.bowesrailway.co.uk

One of the earliest railways in the world. Linked to George Stephenson, and has much of interest to anyone with North-East railway ancestry.

LAING ART GALLERY
New Bridge Street, Newcastle upon Tyne NE1 8AG
Tel: 0191 232 7734
Email: laing@twmuseums.org.uk
www.twmuseums.org.uk/laing

Many exhibits of interest in reference to Tyneside social history.

SHIPLEY ART GALLERY
Prince Consort Road, Gateshead NE8 4JB
Tel: 0191 477 1495
Email: shipley@twmuseums.org.uk
www.twmuseums.org.uk/shipley

Social History through art and displays the painting *The Blaydon Races*.

SOUTER LIGHTHOUSE
Coast Road, Whitburn SR6 7NH
Tel: 0191 529 3161
Email: souter@nationaltrust.org.uk
www.nationaltrust.org.uk

Of interest to anyone with a maritime background, coastal or otherwise, and has fine views across the region.

THE CUSTOMS HOUSE
Mill Dam, South Shields NE33 1ES
Tel: 0191 454 1234
Email: mail@customshouse.co.uk
www.customshouse.co.uk

Now a theatre but worth a visit if you are on the maritime trail.

Wearside

SUNDERLAND MUSEUM AND WINTER GARDENS
Burdon Road, Sunderland SR1 1PP
Tel: 0191 553 2323
Email: sunderland@twmuseums.org.uk
www.twmuseums.org.uk/sunderland

A number of rooms dedicated to the industries important to Wearside and an impressive room featuring local pottery. Mowbray Park, outside, contains material related to the Victoria Hall Disaster, Jack Crawford, and Henry Havelock, a British commander during the Indian Mutiny.

THE NATIONAL GLASS CENTRE
Liberty Way, Sunderland SR6 0GL
Tel: 0191 515 5555
Email: info@nationalglasscentre.com
www.nationalglasscentre.com

Has many contemporary features and includes a Glass Tour describing the history of glassmaking in Sunderland.

SUNDERLAND MARITIME HERITAGE
Unit 2, Church Street East, East End, Sunderland SR1 2BB
Tel: 0191 510 2540
Email: via website
www.sunderlandmaritimeheritage.org.uk

Dedicated to the preservation and conservation of all to do with the maritime heritage of Sunderland (shipping and shipbuilding).

FULWELL WINDMILL
Newcastle Road, Fulwell, Sunderland SR5 1EX
Tel: 0191 516 9790
Email: fulwell.windmill@sunderland.gov.uk
 www.fulwell-windmill.com

Opening times may vary so consult first. Also useful for picking up a Millers' Trail Leaflet (see chapter 3, Agriculture).

WASHINGTON F PIT MUSEUM
Albany Way, Washington, Sunderland, NE37 1BJ
www.twmuseums.org.uk

Only opens occasionally but is an interesting resource for anyone with ancestors who worked with stationary colliery engines – contact the Museum Service for details.

The winding engine – Washington F Pit Museum.

WASHINGTON OLD HALL
The Avenue, Washington Village, Washington NE38 7LE
Tel: 0191 416 6879
Email washington.oldhall@nationaltrust.org.uk
www.nationaltrust.org.uk

Manor house associated with the family of George Washington but of interest to all with Washington connections, from the seventeenth century to date.

MONKWEARMOUTH STATION MUSEUM
North Bridge Street, Sunderland SR5 1AP
Tel: 0191 567 7075
Email: monkwearmouth@twmuseums.org.uk
www.twmuseums.org.uk

Undergoing considerable refurbishment and may have a change of name on reopening. Dedicated to the social history of all forms of transport in the North-East with special reference to Wearside.

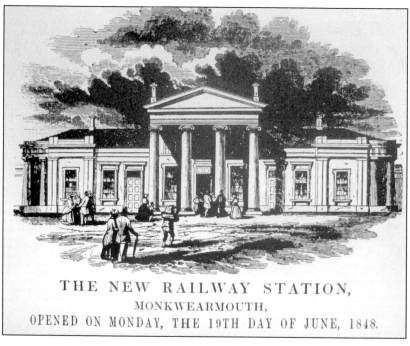

THE NEW RAILWAY STATION,
MONKWEARMOUTH,
OPENED ON MONDAY, THE 19TH DAY OF JUNE, 1848.

Railway station to museum – Monkwearmouth.

Modern County Durham

BEAMISH NORTH OF ENGLAND OPEN AIR MUSEUM
Beamish, County Durham DH9 0RG
Tel: 0191 370 4000
Email: museum@beamish.org.uk
www.beamish.org.uk – also accesses collections

This is a substantial museum of international standing, which features extensively in the text. A must for anyone with roots in the North-East, in particular, it also appears in the Archives and Library sections.

Beamish also maintains the Regional Museums store – which is a joint venture with Tyne and Wear Museums – a huge warehouse storing objects not on show, such as a twentieth-century Tyne wherry boat and a late-twentieth-century Doxford marine engine.

DURHAM LIGHT INFANTRY MUSEUM AND ART GALLERY
Aykley Heads, Durham City DH1 5TU
Tel: 0191 384 2214
Email: dli@durham.gov.uk
www.durham.gov.uk/dli

Medal room and exhibits on the way 'the Durhams lived and died' offering many specialised meetings and talks. Excellent and informative website.

DURHAM HERITAGE CENTRE AND MUSEUM
St Mary-le-Bow, North Bailey, Durham DH1 5ET
Tel: 0191 384 5589
http://web.ukonline.co.uk/durhamheritagecentre

Display of Durham history from Saxon times right up to the present day featuring hands-on material and some temporary exhibitions.

KILLHOPE NORTH OF ENGLAND LEAD MINING MUSEUM
Near Cowshill, Upper Weardale, Co. Durham DL13 1AR
Tel: 01388 537 505
Email: killhope@durham.gov.uk
www.durham.gov.uk/killhope

Features all the aspects of life of the Durham lead miner – a national-award-winner – and many regular activities.

LOCOMOTION: THE NATIONAL RAILWAY MUSEUM AT SHILDON
Shildon, Co Durham DL4 1PQ
Tel: 01388 777999
www.locomotion.uk.com

Celebrates one of the world's oldest railway towns and has an original locomotive, which took part in the famous Rainhill Trials.

TANFIELD RAILWAY
Andrews House, Sunniside, Gateshead NE16 5ET
www.tanfield-railway.co.uk

Oldest part dates back to the seventeenth century. Passenger trains run from time to time – check for details. See website for most current contact details.

HARPERLEY PRISONER OF WAR CAMP
Firtree, Crook, County Durham, DL15 8DX
Tel: 01388 767098
www.powcamp.com

Of interest to those whose families were prisoners of war in North-East England.

ANKER'S HOUSE MUSEUM
Church Chare, Chester-le-Street DH3 3QB
Tel: 0191 388 3295

Much early material but also relates to the later history of the town.

WEARDALE MUSEUM AT HIGH HOUSE CHAPEL
Ireshopeburn, Weardale DL13 1HD
http://www.weardalemuseum.co.uk

Methodism, local social history and copies of the census for Stanhope parish 1841–1901. See website for most current details.

DERWENTCOTE STEEL FURNACE
Forge Lane, Hamsterley, Rowlands Gill, Tyne and Wear, NE39 1BA
www.derwentside.gov.uk

Open one day a week during the summer months – see leisure and culture/local history and heritage section of the website.

Tees Valley

DARLINGTON RAILWAY CENTRE AND MUSEUM

North Road Station, Darlington DL3 6ST
Tel: 01325 460532
Email: museum@darlington.gov.uk
www.drcm.org.uk

Boasts 'the world's most important group of early railway buildings'.

STOCKTON GREEN DRAGON MUSEUM AND ART GALLERY

Theatre Yard, Calverts Lane, Stockton TS18 1JZ
Tel: 01642 527982
Email: greendragonstudios@teesmusicalliance.co.uk
www.stockton.gov.uk/museums

Located among historic warehouses – photography recording the history of Stockton and district.

PRESTON HALL MUSEUM

Preston Park, Yarm Road, Stockton TS18 3RH
Tel: 01642 527375
Email: PrestonHall@stockton.gov.uk
www.stockton.gov.uk/museums

Of interest to anyone with ancestry in nineteenth- or twentieth-century Stockton.

MUSEUM OF HARTLEPOOL

Maritime Avenue, Hartlepool TS24 0XZ
Tel: 01429 860077
Email : info@hartlepoolsmaritimeexperience
www.destinationhartlepool.com

Features the bombardment of Hartlepool, and the history of local fishing and industry.

CAPTAIN COOK BIRTHPLACE MUSEUM

Stewart Park, Marton, Middlesbrough TS7 8AT
Tel: 01642 311211
E-mail: capt.cookmuseum@middlesbrough.gov.uk
www.captaincook-ne.org.uk

Eighteenth-century maritime features, mostly involving former Yorkshire areas.

CAPTAIN COOK SCHOOLROOM MUSEUM

101, High Street, Great Ayton TS9 6NB
Tel: 01642 724296
www.captaincookschoolroommuseum.co.uk

HMS BARK ENDEAVOUR

Castlegate Quay, Stockton-on-Tees
Tel: 01642 676844
www.castlegatequay.co.uk

ORMESBY HALL

Church Lane, Ormesby, Middlesbrough TS7 9AS
Tel: 01642 324188
www.nationaltrust.org.uk

Regency and Victorian exhibits and part of a Jacobean House.

DORMAN MUSEUM

Linthorpe Road, Middlesbrough TS5 6LA
Tel: 01642 813781
Email: dormanmuseum@middlesbrough.gov.uk
www.dormanmuseum.co.uk

A wide sweep of history, some of it of local interest.

KIRKLEATHAM MUSEUM, REDCAR

Kirkleatham, Redcar TS10 5NW
Tel: 01642 479500
E-mail: museum_services@redcar-cleveland.gov.uk
www.redcar-cleveland.gov.uk/museums

Includes archives and maritime history.

ZETLAND LIFEBOAT MUSEUM

5, King Street, Redcar TS10 3AH
Tel: 01642 494 311
E-mail: museum_services@redcar-cleveland.gov.uk
www.redcarlifeboat.org.uk/zetland

Includes the world's oldest lifeboat and much on the history of fishing.

GUISBOROUGH MUSEUM

Sunnyfield House, 36,Westgate, Guisborough TS14 6BA
Tel: 01287 634595
E-mail: museum_services@redcar-cleveland.gov.uk
www.redcar-cleveland.gov.uk/museums

Features the social, agricultural and industrial history of the town, and Victorian displays.

TOM LEONARD MINING MUSEUM

Deepdale, Skinningrove, Saltburn TS13 4AP
Tel: 01287 642877
www.ironstonemuseum.co.uk

Covers the mining of ironstone, vital to areas further north in the region in the nineteenth century.

NB

See also p. 168. A number of Heritage sites have signed up to MLA and others are likely to in the future.

SELECT BIBLIOGRAPHY

For the most up-to-date local histories visit the websites of the appropriate library or local studies centre. Most of these websites have excellent updated lists.

For specific genealogical material, contact the local Family History Society or see copies past and present of the monthly Family History magazines such as *Ancestors, Your Family Tree* and *Family History Monthly.*

Allan, Thomas. *Tyneside Songs* (1862, reprint Frank Graham, Newcastle upon Tyne 1972)

Anderson, K (compiler). *What Is Coal?* (Partnership Project, Seaham 2005)

Atkinson, Frank. *Victorian Britain: The North East* (David and Charles, Newton Abbot 1989)

Barrow, Tony. *Trafalgar Geordies And North Country Seamen of Nelson's Navy 1793–1815* (North East Press, Sunderland 2005)

Bell, David and Patterson, Edwin. *Curious Characters of Lakeland* (Oriel Press, Newcastle upon Tyne 1970)

Bellerby, Rachel. *Tracing Your Yorkshire Ancestors* (Pen & Sword Books, Barnsley, 2006)

Bewick, Thomas. *My Life* (The Folio Society, London 1981 reprint)

Blake, Joyce and Brian. *The Story of Carlisle* (Eyre and Spottiswoode, London 1958)

Bragg, Melvyn. *Speak for England* (Secker and Warburg, London 1976)

Conduit, Brian. *Battlefield Walks Northumbria and the Scottish Borders* (Sigma Leisure, Wilmslow 2005)

Clarke, Joe. *Building Ships On The North East Coast, Pts 1 and 2* (Bewick, Whitley Bay 1997)

Creber, Maeve. *A Sundered Land* (Livres Printemps, Exeter 2006)

Crickmer, Clive. *Grass Roots: A History of South Shields Cricket Club 1850–1984* (The Cricket Club, South Shields 1985)

Cumbria Archives. Cumbrian Ancestors: Notes for Genealogical Researchers 3rd edn (1998)

Curtis, Jack. *Sunderland: A River of Life* (People's History 2003)

Dewdney, J C (ed). *Durham County and City With Teesside* (Library Association, London 1973)

Dobson, Scott and Miller, Ken. *The New Little Broon Book* (Bridge Studios, Berwick upon Tweed 1990)

Dougan, D. *A History of North East Shipbuilding* (Allen and Unwin, London 1968)

Fordyce, W. *History of Durham* (Fullarton, Newcastle 1857)

Fraser, C M and Emsley, K. *Tyneside* (David and Charles, Newton Abbot 1973)

Garson, William S. *The Romance of Old Tynemouth* (The Northern Press, North Shields 1934)

Garson, William S. *Tynemouth's Prominence in Lifeboat History* (The Northern Press, North Shields 1934)

Gibbon, William M. *A Change of Scene: A Nostalgic Appreciation of Barrow's Theatres and Cinemas* (Author, Barrow-in-Furness 1986)

Graham, Frank. *Famous Northern Battles* (Frank Graham, Newcastle upon Tyne 1976)

Gray, Hilary (Ed). *A Celebration of 40 years of Cumbria Lake District Life* (Pelham, London 1991)

Gregson, Keith. *Corvan: A Victorian Entertainer and His Songs* (Kemble, Oxford 1983)

Grigg, R. *The Principal Inhabitants of Cumberland and Westmorland with Furness and Cartmel 1829* (Beewood Coldell, Warrington 1988)

Hannan, Norman. *Travels and Heartaches of a Mining Family* (Author, Romford 1984)

Hartlepool Borough Council. *History of Hartlepools Merger Booklet* (1967)

Histon, Vanessa. *Unlocking the Quayside: Newcastle Gateshead's Historic Waterfront Explored* (Tyne Bridge Publishing, Newcastle upon Tyne 2006)

House, J W and Fullerton, B. *Teesside At Mid Century* (Macmillan, London 1960)

Huggins, Michael and Walton, John K. *The Teesside Seaside between the Wars: Redcar and its Neighbours, 1919–1938* (NEHI, Middlesbrough 2003)

Ireland, Minna. *Elwick: A Thousand Years in the Life of a Village* (Private, 2001)

Judge, Edward T. *Dorman Long: A Concise History* (Private, Teesside 1992)

Keys, Richard E. *Dictionary of Tyne Sailing Ships: A Record of merchant sailing ships owned, registered and built in the port of Tyne from 1830–1930* (Author 1998)

Lakescene Publications. *Guide to Carlisle* (Carlisle N.D. 1970s)

Lillie, W. *History of Middlesbrough* (County Borough Council, Middlesbrough 1968)

Lockett, Alan. *The Man Wants His Boat: Stories of Barrow Shipyard* (1995)

Mains, Brian and Tuck, Anthony. *Royal Grammar School, Newcastle Upon Tyne: A History of the School in its Community* (Oriel Press, Stocksfield 1986)

Marshall J D, and Davies-Shiel, M. *The Lake District at Work – Past and Present* (David and Charles, Newton Abbot 1971)

McCord, Norman. *North East England: The Region's Development 1760–1960* (Batsford, London 1979)

Milburn, G E. *The Christian Lay Churches: Their Origins and Progress* (Independent Methodist Church, Sunderland 1977)

Miller, Edwin (compiler). *Eyewitness: The Industrial Revolution in the North East* (Harold Hill, Sunderland 1967)

Miller, F. *Under Shell Fire* (Hartlepool 1924)

Mountford, Colin E. *The Private Railways of County Durham* (Industrial Railway Society, Melton Mowbray 2004)

Myers, Bill. *Millom Remembered* (Tempus, Stroud 2004)

Pinchbeck, Ivy. *Women Workers and the Industrial Revolution 1750–1850* (2nd edn Virago, London 1968)

Redfern, Barry. *Victorian Villains: Prisoners from Newcastle Gaol 1871–1873 (2006)*

Richardson, M. *Durham People in Old Photographs* (Sutton, Stroud 2004)

Richmond, T. *Local Records of Stockton and Neighbourhood* (Robinson, Stockton 1868)

Rose, Michael E. *The Poor and the City: The English Poor Law in its Urban Context* (The University Press, Leicester 1985)

Runciman, Walter. *Collier Brigs and Their Sailors* (1926 & Conway Maritime Press, London 1971)

Senior, A. *The Folks Alang the Road (Author, Wallsend 1980)*

Sinclair, Neil. *Sunderland, City and People Since 1945* (Breedon, Derby 2004)

Trescatheric, B. *A Centenary History of the Town Hall of Barrow-in-Furness 1887–1987* (Titus Wilson, Kendal 1987)

Trescatheric, B. *Roose, A Cornish Village in Furness* (Hougenai Press, Barrow-in-Furness 1983)

Turnbull, L. *The History of Lead Mining in the North East of England* (Hill, Newcastle 1975)

Wainwright, A. *A Second Furness Sketchbook* (Westmorland Gazette, Kendal 1979)

Wilson, Joe. *Tyneside Songs* and Drolleries (S R Publishers, Wakefield 1970 reprint)

Wood, R. *West Hartlepool* (The Borough, Hartlepool 1969)

Woodhouse, Robert. *County Durham: Strange but True* (Sutton, Stroud 2004)

OTHER RECOMMENDED BOOKS ON GENEALOGY IN GENERAL:

Colwell, S. *Family Roots* (Weidenfeld and Nicholson, London 1991)

Herbor, M D. *Ancestral Trails* (Sutton, Stroud 1999)

Higgs, E. *A Clear Sense of the Census* (1996)

Pevsner, Nikolaus. *The Buildings of England* (various county guides, original and re-edited)

Shell County Guides

Victoria County Histories (various)

INDEX

Addison, Mrs 118
Adelaide 38
Aden 145
Affleck, Cissie 183,
Afghanistan 105
Africa 145
Agricultural Gazette 160
Allendale 4, 26, 89, 97
Allenhead 4
Alnmouth 5, 73, 144
Alnwick, vii, 4, 20, 47, 66, 70, 89, 102, 132, 137, 180, 182
Alnwick Castle and Museum 115, 180
Alnwick Infirmary 102
Alston 3, 26, 29, 50, 89, 147, 178
Amalgamated Society of Woodworkers 157
Amberley Castle 40
Amble 73
Ambleside 3, 121
America 2, 85, 147, 148
Amsterdam 62
Anderson, Robert 46, 75, 76, 78, 118, 133
Anick Common 27
Anker's House Museum 188
Annand, Richard 107
Anthorn 111
Appleby 3, 50, 155
Argosy Steamship Company 69
Armstrong, Jack 137
Armstrong, Tommy 23, 121, 128
Armstrong's 35, 40, 100
Ashbrooke 45, 129
Ashbrooke and Beyond, To 135
Ashby and Jeffrey 44
Ashington 4, 29, 136, 156, 157, 181,
Asia 146
Aspatria 130,
Atkinson, George William 101
Atkinson, Lancelot 74
Austin 37, 38, 40
Austin Pickersgill 38
Australia 45, 63, 129, 147
Awdry, W 54
Ayresome Ironworks 57
Ayton (author) 20

Backbarrow 52, 54, 57
Backhouse family 86
Bacon family 148,
Bailiffgate Museum 70, 180
Bakewell, Robert 48
Balhambra's 134
Ball, Alexander 121
Ballast Hills 102
Baltic region 146
Baltimore 86, 148
Bamburgh 5, 179
Barnard Castle 11, 50, 118, 130
Barrow-in-Furness vii, 3, 13, 27, 31, 33, 35, 36, 40, 42, 49, 52, 53, 57, 58, 61, 69, 101, 109, 110, 111, 112, 113, 122, 129, 130, 137, 143, 144, 145, 154, 155, 162
Barrow-in-Furness Dock Museum 42, 58, 70, 72, 136, 174
Barrow News 155
Barrow Steelworks 58
Barrow, Tony 114
Bartram 38
Bassenthwaite 3, 78
Beacon, The 177
Beadnell 73
Beamish 30, 50, 53, 123, 187
Beamish North of England Open Air Museum 50, 70, 72, 123, 160, 187
Bede 83, 117
Bede School 122
Bedlington 4, 20
Bedlington Ironworks 57
Bek, Bishop 50
Bel-air 148
Belford 102
Belgian Refugee Community 91, 146, 163
Bell Bros 77
Bell Family 35
Bell, Thomas and Sons 57
Bellingham 4, 102
Bellingham Heritage Centre 29, 172
Benfieldside 91
Bennett 142
Benwell 28

Berwick Borough Museum 178
Berwick Parish Church 180
Berwick Rangers 12
Berwick Town Walls 180,
Berwick-upon-Tweed 4, 5, 49, 57, 62, 86, 89, 93, 96, 97, 102, 109, 110, 115, 144, 156, 157, 178, 18
Bessemer 52, 53, 145
Bewcastle 49
Bewick Thomas 4, 50, 181
Bewley, Joseph 76, 133
Billingham 12, 77, 92
Billy 70
'Billy Boy' 127, 128
Birmingham 64
Birtley 91, 146
Biscop, Benedict 83
Bishop Auckland 11, 91, 129
Bishopwearmouth 9, 69, 90, 93, 101, 103
Bishopwearmouth Iron Company 57
Bittlestone, Lewis 101
Black, William 49
Blackburn 145
Black Country 33, 145
Blackhall 11, 17
Blackpool 3
Bladen, Thomas 148
Blair, Tony 11
Blamire, Susanna 76, 119
Blandford House 157, 182
Blaydon 90
'Blaydon Races, The' 8, 35, 59, 133, 134, 183
Blyth 4, 63, 114
Blyth Local Studies Library 89, 97, 162
Blyth Spartans 129, 162
Boer War 108, 113
Bolckow, Henry 52, 55
Boldon 7, 90
Boldon Book 7
Boldon Colliery 7
Bolton 145
Border Regiment 105, 107, 108, 114, 177
Borneo 107, 116
Borrowdale 27, 29, 178
Bounty 71, 111
Bowes (Tyneside) 60
Bowes, John 33

Bowes Museum 11
Bowes Railway 70, 183
Bowman, Joe 131, 132
Bowness (Solway) 73
Bradford 85
Braithwaite's Woollen Manufacturers 79
Brampton 2, 50, 131
Breage 27
Brierton 48
Brigflatts Meeting House 85
Bristol 64, 111
British Medical Association 157
British Oxygen 77
British Steel Corporation 57
British Titan 77
Brocklebank, Daniel 35
Brown, Jackie 133
Bruce's Academy 118
Brus (de) 48
Buccleuch, Duke of 27, 57
Bunny, John 26
Burdon 9
Burgh-by-Sands 3, 119
Burma 108
Burnikell, Richard 69
Burra 143
Buttermere 29
Byker 6
Bywell 173

Calcutta 144,
Caldbeck 26, 76
'Caldbeck Wedding, The' 133
Calder Hall 2, 77
Cambridge 11
Cameron's Strongarm 128
Camperdown 65
Canada 32, 45, 63, 147
Captain Cook Schoolroom Museum 123, 190
Cargo Fleet 57
Caribbean 72, 127,
Carling Will 130
Carlisle vii, 2, 5, 40, 46, 49, 60, 61, 62, 64, 66, 67, 75, 79, 85, 88, 92, 99, 100, 101, 104, 114, 117, 121, 122, 134, 149, 154, 162, 175, 177
Carlisle Airport 115, 175
Carlisle Bell 130

Carlisle Castle 108, 114, 154, 177
Carlisle Cathedral 88
Carlisle Grammar School 117
Carlisle Journal 155
Carlisle United 129, 135
Carpathia 42, 111
Carter, Raich 136
Cartmel, 3, 131, 155
Castle Eden 100
Castle Eden Brewery 128
Castle Ward 102
Causey Arch 71
Cavendish 3
Centre for Life 136
Challenger 38
Chamberlain 5
Chambers, Bob 131
Chantry Bagpipe Museum 136, 181
Charlie, Bonny Prince 2
Charlton 5, 136
Chathill 115, 180
Cherryburn 4, 50, 181
Cheshire 155,
Chester 88
Chester-le-Street 11, 22, 65, 66, 188
Cheviots 156
Chillingham 89
China 40
Christian, Fletcher 71, 111
Churches Conservation Trust 173
City of Adelaide 39
Clanny (lamp) 19
Clark Chapman 41
Clasper, Harry 131, 133
Claypath 91
Cleadon 46
Cleadon Mill 46
Cleator Moor 26
Cleveland 12, 13, 27, 52
Cleveland Railway 67
Cleveland Salt Company 77
Clifford, Lady Anne 155,
Clifton Moor 105
Clough, Tom 137
Clyde 35, 37
Coal 2
Coalbrookdale 52
Coal Mining Oral History Project 28, 165
Cockermouth 3, 101, 111, 155
Cockin, Canon 101
Cockton Hill 91
Coffee Johnny 133
Coldstream 86
Coleman, Terry 147
Colossus 114
Collings 48
Collingwood, Admiral Lord Cuthbert 4, 111, 118
Common Bros 69

Concorde 9
Coniston 3, 25, 26, 27, 78, 86, 142
Connaught 60
Conrad, Joseph 39
Consett 11, 55, 58
Cook, James 72, 123, 189
Cookson, Catherine 115, 182, 183
Cookson, Catherine Trail 182
Cookson's 74, 79
Copeland, Deanery 89
Corbridge 4
Corder manuscripts 41, 91, 164
Cornforth 96
Cornwall 17, 27, 85, 128, 142, 142
Corstopitum 4
Cort, Henry 52
Corvan, Ned 133, 145, 147
Cotherstone 11
County Durham Libraries 28
Cow'd-lword 127
Cowpen 27
Cox Green 38
Cramlington 4, 20
Craster 5, 73
Crawford, Jack 65, 111, 164, 184
Crickmer, Clive 135
Crimean War 106, 108, 113
Croft 67
Cromwell, Oliver 2, 11
Crook 91, 129, 188
Crosthwaite 44
Crowdy 127
Crowley, Ambrose 52
Crowley's 55
Croxdale 91
Crystal Palace 75
Cullercoats 7, 73, 74, 170
Culley family 49
Culley, George 49
Cumberland 2, 3, 44, 46, 75, 102, 125, 127, 129, 131, 132, 136, 144, 154, 155, 157, 159
Cumberland and Westmorland Constabulary 101
Cumberland and Westmorland Regiments 107, 108
Cumberland and Westmorland Volunteers 107
Cumberland Infirmary 99
Cumberland Pacquet 155
Cumberland Pencil Museum 175
Cumberland United Steel 57
Cumbria Archives 27, 40, 49, 57, 67, 69, 79, 88, 89,

96, 101, 113, 122, 155, 172
Cumbria Family History Society 172
Curwen 40, 57
Customs House 184
Cuthbert, Saint 10, 11, 83, 117

Dalston 101, 122
Dalton 3, 26, 101, 144
Dalton, Mary 75, 76,
Darling, Grace Museum 179
Darlington 12, 13, 44, 48, 50, 66, 67, 76, 86, 92, 97, 103, 129, 143, 159, 165, 189
Darlington Centre for Local Studies 92, 97, 103, 165
Darlington Railway Centre and Museum 189
Date family 142
Davy (Lamp) 19
Deaf Hill 122
Dent 66, 75, 155
Denton 6
Denton, Gray and William Gray 39
Deptford (Wear) 38
Derry 60
Derwent, River 154
Derwentcote Steel Furnace 58, 188
Derwentwater 78
Derwent Valley 26
Devon 25, 27, 85, 142
Dickens, Charles 11, 118
Discovery Museum 30, 42, 72, 79, 80, 104, 115, 136, 137, 157, 182
Dixon, Michael 100
Dixon's Chimney 75
Doidge 142
Dolan family 80
Dolgoch 54
Domesday Book 7
Donnison School 120
Dorman Long 55, 56
Dorman Museum 58, 71, 80, 116
Dotheboys Hall 118
Dove Cottage 49, 176
Doxford 37, 38, 40, 144, 187
Dublin 62
Duddon Bridge 54
Duddon, River 154
Dudley 33, 145
Duglison family 148
Duke Pit 20
Dumbarton 33
Duncansclett 143
Dundee 143
Dunn, Ann 96
Dunn, John 137

Dunstanburgh 5
Dunston Engine Works Company 56
Durham Advertiser 160
Durham, Bishop of 105
Durham Cathedral 83, 167
Durham Chronicle 165
Durham City 10, 11, 24, 50, 60, 66, 76, 92, 100, 130, 187
Durham Clayport Library 165
Durham Community Heritage Project 165
Durham County Advertiser 165
Durham County Libraries 165
Durham County Record Office 89, 90, 91, 92, 97, 103, 114, 122, 158,159
Durham Heritage Centre and Museum 187
Durham Iron and Steel Company 56
Durham Light Infantry 105, 106, 114, 116, 159, 187
Durham Light Infantry Museum and Art Gallery 115, 116, 187
Durham Miner Project 28, 165
Durham Pals 107
Durham School 118, 130
Durham Tees Valley Airport 111
Durham University 121, 167

Eamont 67
Earsdon 20
Easington 11, 17, 22, 23
East Boldon 7, 90
East Stanley 123
Edinburgh 66, 76
Eden 132
Eden, Robert 148
Efficient 41
Egglescliffe 96
Egglescliffe Chemical Company 77
Egremont 26, 178
El Alamein 106
Eldon, Lord 118
Elisabethville 91, 146
Ellen, River 35
Ellingham 156
Ellington Colliery 20
Elliot, Billy 1,
Elpis 63
Elswick 6, 35, 42, 173
Elwick 48
Embleton 102,
Empire Theatre 134
Eppleton 9
Errington, Edward 27
Escomb 92

Eskdale Mill 49, 178
Eston 91
Etal 5, 179
Ewart 49

F Pit Museum 30, 87, 115, 185
Falmouth 144
Farfield Mill 49, 80, 174
Farmers' Guardian 160
FARNE (Folk Archive Resource North East) 167, 170
Fell family 85, 86
Fell, William 85, 148
Felling 21, 28, 79, 90, 159
Felling Chemical Company 57
Fell's Point 86, 148
Felton 89
Fenwick 5
Ferguson family 75
Fleet Air Arm 111
Fleetwith Pike 29
Fleetwood 143
Fleming, Daniel 155
Flinters Gill 66
Florence Mine Heritage Centre 29, 178
Ford(Northumberland) 5, 49, 57, 179
Ford (Wearside) 9
Foster 5
Fowberry 49
Fox, George 85
Friar's Goose 79
Friend family 142
Friends School 122
Frosterley 11
Fulwell 9, 46
Fulwell Mill 46, 185, Furness 2, 3, 17, 26, 53, 57, 85, 88, 155, 174
Furness Abbey 51, 92
Furness, Christopher 56, 93
Furness Railway 61
Fusiliers Museum of Northumberland 180

Gallipoli 108
Galloway 18
Garigill 89
Gateshead 5, 6, 8, 21, 53, 56, 57, 67, 70, 77, 88, 89, 90, 100, 102, 122, 129, 146, 158, 159, 163, 183, 188
Gateshead Central Library 90, 97, 163
Gateshead Iron Company 56
Gateshead Observer 163
Gateshead Park Ironworks 57
Geordie 5, 66, 67, 126
George V, King 67
Germany 56, 116

Gibbon, William 137
Gibbs, Dr 133
Gibson, Alexander Craig, 125
Gilchrist-Thomas, Sidney 53
Gladstone 121
Glasgow 66
Glendale 102
Gosforth (Tyneside) 6, 66, 97, 130, 156
Graf Spee 111
Grange-over-Sands 3
Grasmere 3, 176
Grasslot 61
Gray family 5
Gray, Rector Society 173
Great Ayton 13, 123, 190
Great Orton 46
Green Howards 109
Greenwich 31, 62
Green Dragon Museum 72, 80, 116, 189
Gregg family 142
Gregg, Thomas 86, 87
Gregson, Betty (see Stephens)
Gregson, George 33
Gregson, Harold 111
Gretna Green 86
Grey, Earl 95
Guildhall Museum 104
Guisborough 13, 19, Guisborough Museum 191
Gurney, Bobby 136

Hackworth, Timothy 61, 71
Hadrian's Wall 1, 7, 67
Haggerston 89
Haig Colliery Mining Museum 29, 175
Hall Bros 69
Hall, Jean 99
Haltwhistle 4, 102, 171
Hamsterley 58
Hannigan, Kate 183
Harperley POW Camp Heritage Site 116, 188, Hardy's (Shop and Museum) 132, 137, 182
Harrington 79
Harrington Chemical Works 79
Harrison, Paul 135
Hart 92
Hart Jackson and Son 57
Hartlepool, vii, 1, 12, 13, 31, 39, 41, 42, 48, 50, 53, 60, 61, 62, 72, 73, 77, 91, 92, 93, 99, 100, 110, 112, 116, 122 129, 134, 144, 159, 166, 171, 189
Hartlepool Historic Quay 116
Hartlepool Local Studies Library 97

Hartlepool Mail 166
Hartlepool, Museum of 42, 58, 72, 116, 137, 189
Hartlepool Reference Library 166
Hartlepool Rovers 130
Hartlepools 12, 40, 61, 70, 85, 109, 166
Hartlepools, Bombardment of 112, 166
Hartley's 74, 75, 79
Haughey, Edward Solway Aviation Museum 175
Haughton-Le-Skerne 103
Havelock, Henry 184
Haverton Hill Shipyard 42
Hawks, Crawshay and Co. 56, 57
Hawthorn Leslie 41
Hay and Company 39
Haydon Bridge 4, 89
Hazlehurst, Isaac 92
Head Wrightson 56, 57
Heathcotes (Cleator Moor) Ltd 57
Heatherslaw Corn Mill 179
Hebburn 7, 31, 42, 56, 77, 90, 159
Hedgehog Pie 128
Hedley, William 61
Henry VIII 118
Her Majesty's Theatre 134
HMS *Bark Endeavour* 190
Heron family 5
Herrington 21
Hetton-le Hole 9, 17, 103
Heugh Battery 116
Heworth 79, 90
Hexham 1, 4, 5, 44, 92, 96, 97, 102, 162, 181
Hexham Local Studies Library 89, 97, 102, 162
Hexham Old Gaol 181
Hexhamshire 4
Heysham 3, 50
High Carley 101
High Furness 125
High House Chapel 85, 93, 188
High Level Bridge 56, 67, 118
Hillside Cemetery 22, 93, 173
Hilton family 148
Hine family 87
Hinks 44
Hodbarrow Mine 26, 27, 54, 144, 154
Hodgson family 4
Hodgson, David 86
Hodgson, Richard 119
Holland 108
Hollywood 135
Holme Shipping Line 63, 87
Holmrook 178

Honister 27
Honister Slate Museum 29, 178
Horden 11, 17
Horetop 142
Horn, Walter 75
Hornsby 44
Houghton-le-Spring 9, 17, 22, 90, 93, 102, 173
Holy Island (see Lindisfarne)
Hudderson, Nicholas 19
Hudleston 49
Hudson, George 62
Hughes 33
Hughes, Job 145
Hull 64
Huntley, Phil 47
Huntsman 53
Hutton 43
Hutton John 49
Huwood Mining Machinery Company 160
Hylton 9, 38, 39, 111, 148
Hylton Castle 148

Imperial Chemical Industries 77, 160
Imperial War Museum 116
India 105, 129, 145
Indian Mutiny 184
Ireland 73, 85, 105, 128, 144, 145
Ireshopeburn 188
Ismay, Thomas Henry 63, 71
Italy 116

Jackson, Ralph Ward 62
James 45
James family 148
Jane Pit 20
Japan 40
Jarrow 7, 33, 40, 41, 70, 77, 90, 92, 159
Jarrow March Collection 163
Jesmond 6
Jewish Communities 146
Johnston, W T 75
Joicey 30
Jones, John Paul 111

Kayll, Joe 101
Keegan, Frank 23
Keegan, Kevin 23
Keelman's Hospital 102
Kendal vii, 3, 46, 49, 64, 66, 75, 79, 80, 88, 93, 101, 122, 148, 154, 155, 162, 174
Kendal Chronicle/Mercury 155
Kentmere 27
Kenton 6

Keswick 3, 26, 29, 50, 113, 148, 154, 175, 178
Keswick Museum and Art Gallery 80, 175
Keys, Richard 32, 33
Kielder 4
Killhope 30, 187
Killhope North of England Lead Mining Museum 30, 187
Killingworth 90
King's College 121
King's Liverpool Rifles 109
Kings Lynn 73, 143,
King's Own Border Regiment 107, 108, 114, 177
King's Own Scottish Borderers 109, 178
King's Royal Hussars 109, 115
Kirkby Lonsdale 3, 50
Kirkby Stephen 1, 3, 50
Kirkleatham 13, 190
Kirkleatham Museum 190
Knight, Thomas Memorial Hospital 114
Korea 40, 106, 107

Lads in Blue, The 135
Laing 38, 41
Laing Art Gallery 183
Laing, James 38, 39
Laird family 143
Laird, James 19
Lake District 2, 3, 17, 26, 43, 49, 61, 77, 125, 142
Lakeland Life, Museum 49, 80, 174
Lambton 106, Lambton Coke Works 59
Lamesley 102
Lancashire vii, 1, 2, 3, 51, 66, 96, 109, 111, 121, 125, 130, 145, 155
Lancaster and Penrith Railway 60
Lascars 145
Laurel, Stan 135
Leeds 64, 84
Leeds to Liverpool Canal 64
Lerwick 143
Lesbury 89
Liddell, Joseph 44, 45, 67, 132, 134, 147
Lilburne, John 118
Lindal-in-Furness 26
Lindale 52
Lindisfarne 5, 83, 144
Lithuania 91
Liverpool 2, 35, 112, 145
Living History North East 173
Locomotion No 1 61
Locomotion, National

Railway Museum at Shildon 71, 188
Lodge, George 96
Loftus 30
London 12, 40, 65, 75, 76, 114, 126, 172
Londonderry, Lord 64
Longbenton 90, 118
Longsleddale 27
Longtown 101
Lonsdale, Mark 46
Lord Lucas's Regiment 108
Lorrainers 74
Lowca 54, 61
Lowden Charles G 113
Low Fell 6
Lowick 89, 122
Lowlie, John 49
Lowlie, Jane 49
Ludgvan 27

Macadam 67
'Mackem' 39
Madeley 52
Malaysia 145
Maling, Christopher Thompson 76, 77, 80
Mallory family 148
Manchester 35
Manchester 172
Marr, Earl of 66
Marshall, Catherine 113
Marske 13
Martin 53, 54
Marton 189
Mary Ada 69
Mary, Queen of Scots 2
Maryland 148
Maryport 17, 20, 31, 35, 42, 54, 61, 62, 63, 69, 74, 79, 87, 115, 176
Maryport and Carlisle Railway 61, 67
Maryport Haematite Company 54
Maryport Maritime Museum 42, 71,176
Marytavy 142
Mason, Thomas H 155,
Mauretania 35, 42
McIntosh, Thomas 111
McKenny, Jimmy 134
Mere Knolls 101
Merseyside 77
Metcalfe 67
Middlesbrough 12, 13, 31, 39, 40, 55, 57, 58, 61, 70, 71, 79, 80, 91, 99, 104, 116, 121, 122, 129, 145, 146, 159, 171, 189, 190,
Middlesbrough Reference Library 166
Milburn 5, 136
Milburn, Jackie 136
Millican family 147
Millom vii, 2, 17, 25, 26,

27, 29, 54, 55, 57, 69, 87, 109, 142, 144, 154
Millom and Askham Haematite Iron Co. Ltd 57
Millom Gazette 155
Milvain 34
Mithras 83
Monkhouse family 35
Monkhouse, George 74
Monkwearmouth 9, 21, 61, 90
Monkwearmouth Colliery 121
Monkwearmouth Station Museum 70, 186
Moon, Robert 96
Moorhouse 86
Morecambe 3, 62
Morpeth 4, 55, 66, 79, 89, 97, 100, 102, 111, 136, 156, 162
Morrison, William 22
Mosedale 93
Mountbatten, Lord 111
Mowbray Park 184
Music Hall Museum 137

Napoleonic Wars 108, 110, 134
National Archives, The 28, 49, 68, 161
National Glass Centre 74, 80, 184,
National Maritime Museum 31, 68
National Railway Museum (see Locomotion)
Nelson 111, 114, 116, 118
Nenthead 25, 142, 178
Nenthead Mines Heritage Centre 29, 178
Neville 48
Newbiggin-by-the-Sea 73
New Brunswick 33
New Zealand 45
Newcastle Brown Ale 128
Newcastle Central Station 161, 182
Newcastle Falcons 130
Newcastle Literary and Philosophical Society 118, 167, 168
Newcastle Lying In Hospital 102
Newcastle Racecourse 130
Newcastle Royal Grammar School 112, 118, 123, 130
Newcastle to Carlisle Railway 61
Newcastle Town Moor 130
Newcastle United 129, 133, 136
Newcastle University 166, 167

Newcastle upon Tyne vii, 1, 4, 5, 6, 11, 17, 20, 27, 34, 36, 44, 45, 47, 51, 61, 62, 63, 66, 67, 74, 84, 85, 88, 89, 90, 96, 97, 99, 100, 102, 104, 110, 112, 114, 118, 121, 122, 134, 136, 137, 144, 146, 156, 157, 173, 182, 183
Newcastle upon Tyne Central Library 97, 136, 163
Newton Aycliffe 11, 57
Nicholson, Elizabeth 69
Nicholson, George 96
Nissan 111
Noble, Thomas 43
Norfolk 75
Normanby Iron Works 55
North East Museums, Libraries and Archives Council (NEMLAC) 169
North Elswick Hall 34
North Hylton 75
North of England Museum(see Beamish)
North of England Open Air Museum Regional Resource Centre 160
North of England Lead Mining Museum (see Killhope)
North Sands 38
North Shields 7, 33, 65, 70, 73, 79, 80, 90, 97, 102, 163, 170, 183
North Shields Stag Line 69
North Sunderland 102
North Tyneside 5, 7, 122
North Tyneside Central Library 90, 97, 163,
Northumberland and Durham Family History Society 161, 172
Northumberland and Newcastle Voluntary Cavalry 108
Northumberland Archives (see also Northumberland Collections Service) 27, 29, 57, 67, 79, 86, 88, 89, 90, 92, 96, 97, 102, 113, 122, 156, 157, 171
Northumberland Collections Service 156, 157,
Northumberland Communities Website 79, 171
Northumberland Constabulary 102
Northumberland County Asylum 100, 102
Northumberland, Duke of 20